FOLK MAGIC, SUPERSTITION, AND CHARMS

A COLLECTION

Tarl Warwick

2020

COPYRIGHT AND DISCLAIMER

PREFACE

The purpose of this work is to give a fairly broad overview to folk magic and charms from a variety of works which I have edited over the last half decade. Even in works not dedicated remotely to the topic at hand, a few passages here and there suffice to flesh out the subject matter; in all instances in this work, I have utilized my own self published editions in order to refer the reader to proper and relevant page numbers.

The subject is a vast one. Although I have edited a few dozen works which explicitly relate to the *type* of folklore and magickal practices at hand in this text, I have read at least twice as many which I have not- indeed, it is proper first to say that this present volume had to be artificially limited, specifically because the topic is so vast that ten volumes would be required too even prepare a limited look at the type of lore involved. The genesis of this volume began when I was editing a prior collection of folk medicine and realized that especially in the 18th and 19th centuries, a very large amount of simplistic magick and thousands of charms from manifold cultures were indiscriminately plopped into books (variously, grimoires, receipt books, family physicians, and fortune tellers) which ranged from the mostly academic and rational, to the outright sensational and superstitious.

I have made no real attempt in this volume to differentiate the "believable" folk rites from those of a more fantastic nature- after all, what was believable fifty years ago may often seem to us to be rather odd, and were a person today to relate what is seen as true to someone then, equally so; imagine attempting to explain genetic editing to a person living in the gilded era, and all attempts would seem at best eccentricity and at worst outright madness.

In this work I have deviated from the format which I

generally use, creating subject headers, then referring to the works in question and citing them to each quoted entry. Again, these entries come from my own editions of all works, and therefore may differ from the originals somewhat, as I chose to modernize the English used from what prior to the late 19th century tended to be a rather more archaic form, let alone the form taken prior to the early 19th century, when "Ye olde English" was predominant. The works cited range from grimoires spanning several centuries, to relatively modern folkloric or historical works, and from those which are rather incredulous, to those which are more skeptical of the content and relate it for curiosity or academic study.

The broad nature of the subject allows for multiple sub-categories to be made. I could have decided to categorize the sections according to, say, black and white magick, or according to the era, but finally decided on a pretty basic subcategorical system involved merely with the basic purposes of the rites, lore involving plants or animals, etc. In some cases the content here is a bit more about fortune telling or prognostication than an actual *rite*, per se, but simply consulting a flower or observing an animal is, after all, little more than a folk rite related to some super-mundane purpose.

It should be noted that when speaking of folklore and superstitions involving animals, plants, rocks, etc, I have deliberately chosen not to utilize the term "legend"- why? It is quite simple. A legend, writ large at least in common parlance, is little more than a more elaborate, systematic variant of folklore anyways. Folklore can become legend over time, and legend spawns folklore, but they are in essence little more than one anothers' counterparts, if not complimentary in such a sense that they are inseparable. So we have for example, canonical Catholic ritual and dogma, and then we have a million instances of trinkets, prayers, and rituals which have nothing to do with the commands of a pope, and everything to do with the utilitarian and daily side of life- of using a saint to bless crops, or praying in a certain way to prevent harm during travel. We see this kind of behavior in every religion and legend system. In some Islamic circles, it is held to be a curse if you include a small piece of the Quran cut out and included with a gift you give to a person. This haram practice is nonetheless relatively wide-spread. Amulets to prevent the influence of the evil eye abound in Turkey despite technically being sorcery. Few New England Protestants will nail a decorative horse shoe upside down on the wall.

There is, I argue, no real difference between superstition and folklore on one hand, and legend on the other, except in how it is treated categorically by academics who have been influenced by several generations of post-enlightenment teaching related to the classics; namely, a deep disposition to regard Athens, Rome, Egypt, and so forth, as different from other areas of the world, even in more modern systems. The man who scoffs at another for fearing a black cat crossing their path so often clutches at a lucky rabbits' foot or a crystal, and even self proclaimed mystics and witches may scoff at the crystal ball only to grab their tarot deck!

I have included a little section at the end of this work with some other various occult works which are not cited in this text, for further reading, for those who are seriously interested in the subject.

~Tarl Warwick

CONTENT

FOLK MAGIC

AND CHARMS

PROTECTION AND LUCK CHARMS AND LORE

ANCIENT CURES, CHARMS, AND USAGES OF IRELAND
Lady Wilde, 1890

"The Briar:

Great virtue is attributed to the briar, especially in cases of a sprain, or dislocation; the species bearing a reddish flower being the best for use. A strong twig of this is taken, about a yard long and split evenly from end. to end. The pieces are then held by two men with clean hands, about three feet apart- the mystery-man pronouncing an incantation, and waving his hands over them until the twigs seem endowed with life, and rise up and approach each other till they touch; then a piece is cut off at the point of contact, and bound firmly over the sprain, the mystery-man all the time never ceasing his incantations, nor the waving of his hands. The ligature is left on for three days, after which time the sprain is found to be perfectly cured; but the power of the split sticks is entirely neutralized, should either of the men holding them be illegitimate.

The buds of the briar are used in spring to make a refreshing drink for the sick, and the roots in winter. The roots are boiled for twelve hours in an earthen vessel, then a small cupful of the liquid is administered frequently to the patient, who, after some time, falls into a deep sleep from which he will awake perfectly cured." (p. 47-48.)

"When the body is laid in the coffin, the priest sanctifies a handful of earth and sprinkles it over the corpse. And this is done because, if any self-murdered person were brought to the churchyard to be buried, all the dead would turn in their coffins, unless only those on whose bodies the blessed earth had been sprinkled by the priest. If the face of a first-born child is turned downwards in the coffin, the parents will never have any more children." (p. 54.)

EGYPTIAN SECRETS
L.W DeLaurence, 1900

"When a Man or Cattle is Plagued by Goblins, or Ill-disposed People

Go on Good Friday, or Golden Sunday, ere the sun rise In the East, to a hazelnut bush, cut a stick therefrom with a sympathetic weapon, by making three cuts above the hand toward the rise of the sun, in the name of the t t t Carry the stick noiselessly into the house, conceal it so that no one can get hold of it. When a man or beast is plagued by evil disposed people, walk three times around such a haunted person, while pronouncing the three holiest names; after this proceeding, take off thy hat and hit it with the stick and thus you smite the wicked being." (p. 26.)

"To compel a Thief to return the Stolen Property

Obtain a new earthen pot with a cover, draw water from the under current of a stream while calling out the three holiest names. Fill the vessel one-third, take the same to your home, set it upon the fire, take a piece of bread from the lower crust of a loaf, stick three pins into the bread, boil all in the vessel, add a few dew nettles. Then say: Thief, male or female, bring my stolen articles back, whether thou art boy or girl; thief, if thou art woman or man, I compel thee, in the name, t t t" (p. 28.)

Note that the aforementioned requires, in place of the "t t t" listed, making the sign of the cross thrice.

FOLK MAGIC, SUPERSTITION, AND CHARMS

"A Secret and curious Piece of Marvel, to Discern in a Mirror what an Enemy designs at the Distance of Three Miles or more

Obtain a good plain looking glass, as large as you please, and have it framed on three sides only; upon the left side it should be left open. Such a glass must be held toward the direction where the enemy is existing and you will be able to discern all his markings, maneuverings, his doings and workings. Was effectually used during the thirty years' war." (p. 29.)

"To Cut a Stick wherewith to Punish a Witch that has Attacked the Cattle

Mark well, and observe when the new moon shines on a Tuesday before sunrise, or, perhaps, on a Golden Sunday, which will occur whenever a Friday and Sunday come together, or, perhaps, on Good Friday, also before the rising of the sun, hie thee to a hazelnut bush, which you may have selected beforehand. Stand before the stick toward the rising of the sun, take hold thereof, in the name of God, with both hands, and speak: Stick, I grasp thee, in the name of God the Father, the Son, and the Holy Spirit, that thou shalt be obedient to me, that I may surely hit him whom I design to whip. Whereupon take thy knife, and cut the stick in three cuts, whole pronouncing the three highest names, and carry it quietly to thy home, and guard it well, that no person steals it. If you intend to whip a witch which hath assaulted a beast or human being, go into the reap, house, and pray, before proceeding thence, three times, with great devotion, the article dedicated to the Bedgoblin, (which is the second article in this book), so that she may be destroyed by fire, and no evil spirit may enter into house or stable; otherwise the cats would get madam to scratch the eyes out of your head. Then move round the man or beast so bewitched three times, backward. Now take off the hat, put it upon the floor, and batter so long upon the hat as thou may chose. It will certainly hit the witch; and even if you should hammer holes into your hat, even the witch will then receive holes in his (or her) head. If thou desirest to flog one who is living at a distance from you, who deserves a beating, then place your coat upon a witch's ladder or shears, or upon a threshold, and call the name of him (or her) you design to whip, and you will hit him (or her) just as well as if he (or she) be present. But upon the stick thou must inscribe: 'Abiam, Dabiam, Fabiam. Probatum est!'" (p. 71.)

"When a Witch besets the Animals

Take enzian, juniper berries, ashes of pear tree wood, and salt, of one as much as of the other, of aloes and almond nuts, half the quantity. Pound all pure and fine. Mix well together. After having a pail full of this powder, take a good handful of house leek, and cut it fine. Of this give to the cattle as much as may be taken between three fingers, and push It into their throats. Cut off of such cattle's tail a tuft of hair, so that it may perspire freely. This should be done during the waning of the moon, and treat the animals every morning to a fumigation with juniper berries. Nettle seed mixed with salt is also good at all times." (p. 196.)

ENCHIRIDION OF POPE LEO
1633

"Prayer to Escape Persecutions Including In Criminal Cases

'You, my Lord Jesus, who with your light led the the scribes and the high priest Caiaphas; to you, beloved, that as the savior, you were condemned; You, the Christ, Son of God. I ask that you turn pleading and afflicted, to intercede for this poor sinner, who without reason or cause, was indicted. Be my beam, my Jesus, that light that penetrates the soul of my accusers, not to become cloudy and not to condemn me.

FOLK MAGIC, SUPERSTITION, AND CHARMS

I ask for the precious blood shed by prodigal men, you are Lord, and when you were convicted and you would not defend yourself. + So be it. Blessed Archangels Michael, Raphael and Gabriel, Angels and Cherubim, All Saints, come to my rescue and deliver me from ill will, by God + Almighty. Amen. Amedam, + Austis, + Memor, + Gedita, + Eleison, + Igion, + Frigam, + Fides, + Valey, + Unis, + Regnab, + Saday, + Agios Athanatos, be merciful on me, poor sinner. + So be it.

Blessed Michael the Archangel, + Rafael, Uriel +, + Baraquiel, + Cherubim and Seraphim, + intercede for me. Behold the Cross + of Jesus Christ. Flee, enemies; the lion of the tribe of Judah has overcome; race of David, + hallelujah! Deliver me, my God, from my enemies and those who want to lose. + So be it. Oh, God! Light me with the glory of your holy name and save me and make your righteous power come, showing the goodness and innocence of my cause. + You who have saved the kings and have rescued David, save me from those trying to condemn me unfairly. + So be it. Jesus Christ overcomes, + Jesus Christ reigns, + He is righteous, + He defends me. + Amen.'

Draw the second pentacle with blue ink on parchment or virgin paper of a pure white, on a Monday, starting work at nine o'clock. Wrap then the pentacle with a piece of white silk and take the suspended pentacle and place it about your neck, to recite the prayer. Then you should say three 'Our Fathers' and three 'Hail Marys' in honor and glory of the Holy Trinity."

(p. 19-20.)

Note: The second pentacle follows on the subsequent page: This particular work I cleaned up and modernized from substantially older English.

The protective pentacle.

THE PETIT ALBERT
18th Century

"An Ointment Which Protects Against Fire

There has been for several centuries the custom of using fire to determine the guilt of criminals, but this custom was abolished because it is suspected that it is a way of tempting the Lord. Indeed, it has been discovered, from those times, from ancient historians, the length of time which the accused was suspended in the flames. And here is what I have gathered from the truth on this subject:

To resist flame, make an ointment composed of hibiscus juice, fresh egg, mucous, sphylion seed, powdered lime, and horseradish juice. This is crushed and mixed all together, and rubbed on the whole body, if one will be tested as such, or just on the hands if the person is to be tortured just upon those. The ointment must be allowed to dry onto the body and can be applied as many as three times. This makes the user resistant to all fire." (p. 73-74.)

FOLK MAGIC, SUPERSTITION, AND CHARMS

"The Secret Stick For Travelers

You shall take the day after Halloween a strong branch of elderberry, to be used as a walking stick. Trim the tip off and cap it with an iron cap, and hollow the staff out, removing the core wood inside. Put at the bottom of the hollow stick both eyes of a young wolf, the tongue and heart of a dog, three green lizards, and three swallow hearts. All this to be dried in the sun between two sheets of paper, with the papers dusted with powdered saltpeter. Put above this material in the stick seven verbena leaves, picked the eve of St. John the Baptist, with a stone of various colors, found in the nest of a hoopoe bird, and close up the top of the staff with an whatever material you wish, and be assured that this staff will guarantee you protection from highwaymen, wild beasts, rabid dogs, and venomous snakes. It will also protect you at inns or places where you seek rest, guaranteeing the benevolence of the hosts." (p. 77.)

POW WOWS
John George Hohman, 1822

"To prevent bad people from getting around the cattle

Take wormwood, gith, five-finger weed, and assafoetida; three cents' worth of each; the straw of horse beans, some dirt swept together behind the door of the stable and a little salt. Tie these all up together with a tape, and put the bundle in a hole about the threshold over which your cattle pass in and out, and cover it well with lignumvitae wood. This will certainly be of use." (p. 54.)

"A direction for a gypsy spell, to be carried about the person as a protection under all circumstances

'Like unto the prophet Jonas, as a type of Christ, who was guarded for three days and three nights in the belly of a whale, thus shall the Almighty God, as a Father, guard and protect me from all evil. Jesus, Jesus, Jesus.'" (p. 57.)

"Against evil spirits and all manner of witchcraft

'I.
N. I. R.
I.
SANCTUS SPIRITUS.
I.
N. I. R.
I.

All this be guarded here in time, and there in eternity. Amen.' You must write all the above on a piece of white paper and carry it about you. The characters or letters above signify: 'God bless me here in time, and there eternally.'" (p. 57-58.)

"How to recover stolen goods

Take good care to notice through which door the thief passed out, and cut off three small chips from the posts of that door; then take these three chips to a wagon, unbeshrewdly, however; take off one of the wheels and put the three chips into the stock of the wheel, in the three highest names, then turn the wheel backwards and say:

'Thief, thief, thief! Turn back with the stolen goods; thou art forced to do it by the Almighty power of God: + + + God the Father calls thee back, God the Son turns thee back so that thou must return, and God the Holy Ghost leads thee back, until thou arrive at the place from which thou hast stolen. By the almighty power of God the Father thou must come; by the wisdom of God the Son thou hast neither peace nor quiet until thou hast returned the stolen goods to their former place; by the grace of God the Holy Ghost thou must run and jump and canst find no peace or rest until thou arrivest at the place from which thou hast stolen. God the Father binds thee, God the Son forces thee, and God the Holy Ghost turns thee back. (You must not turn the wheel too fast.) Thief, thou must come, + + + thief, thou must come, + + + thief, thou must come, + + +. If thou art more almighty, thief, thief, thief; if thou art more almighty than God himself, then you may remain where you are. The ten commandments force thee- thou shalt not steal, and therefore thou must come. + + + Amen.'" (p. 75-76.)

SIGNS OMENS AND SUPERSTITIONS
Astra Cielo, 1918.

"Signs of Good or Bad Luck

'Good and ill luck,' says the French philosopher, Montaigne, 'are in my opinion sovereign powers. It is absurd to think that human prudence is able to act the same part as Fortune will do.'

Shakespeare says: 'There's a divinity that shapes our ends, Rough-hew them how will will.'

The belief in the power of some object or some act to produce a change in one's fortunes for better or for worse, is inherent in the human race. There are few words in our language that have such a universal application as LUCK. The man who believes in nothing else, believes in luck and performs some mummery to propitiate the goddess of Fortune, who moves in such mysterious ways to perform her deeds. Luck may be defined as chance, or if a man be religious, as Providence. Among the ancients, Fortuna was depicted as a blindfolded woman with a horn of plenty, or with a wheel as an emblem of instability and chance.

The Romans had a habit of casting into an urn a stone every day, the color of the stone denoting whether the person was in good or bad luck. At the end of the year the stones were counted and a balance cast to see whether good or bad preponderated.

It is unlucky to be recalled after starting away on a voyage. At least a day should be allowed to elapse before starting out again.

To leave home and be compelled to come back for some article which was forgotten, is unlucky, unless you sit down for a moment before going out a second time.

Carrying a crust of bread in one's pocket is considered lucky and brings prosperity. If in eating you miss your mouth and the food falls, it is unlucky and denotes illness.

A bent coin or one with a hole in it, are often carried for good luck. A crooked sixpence is popular for this purpose in England. In many rural districts it is customary to give back to a customer of corn or cattle a small part of the money he has just paid. This is called 'luck money.'

In some countries the buyer gives the seller a small coin to insure his luck. To count your gains is supposed to bring bad luck. To reckon on money you are to receive and lay out plans of spending it, is considered unlucky. One should never count one's chickens before they are hatched.

Burning tea leaves is supposed to bring good luck, but to burn the leaves of a rose is a bad omen. Finding a four-leaf clover is a sure sign of good luck. It should be worn in the lapel or pinned to one's coat.

There is a legend that Eve on being ejected from Paradise took a four-leaf clover with her.

To pluck an ash leaf was considered lucky in olden times.

FOLK MAGIC, SUPERSTITION, AND CHARMS

On meeting a person out on new business, it is well to salute him with 'I wish you good luck.'

It is bad luck to shake hands with any one across the table.

It is a bad omen to find the bellows on the dining table.

It is a sign of ill luck to find money and not spend it. It should be spent in a good cause, or given in charity.

'See a pin and pick it up, all the day you'll have good luck. See a pin and leave it lay, you will have bad luck all the day.'

It is lucky to throw a small coin into a well of drinking water.

To sit cross-legged is considered a sign of good luck. To cross one's fingers is another way of averting evil." (p. 34-35.)

"*Lucky and Unlucky Omens*

'She that pricks bread with fork or knife, will never be a happy wife.'

'Mend your clothes upon your back, sure you are to come to wrack.'

It is unlucky to use elder wood or evergreen to make a fire. To find an old flint arrow is considered lucky.

To find nine peas in a pod is a forerunner of luck.

The extreme tip of a calf's tongue, dried and carried in the pocket, will insure having some money always in your purse.

A luck-stone, with a hole in it, is sure to bring luck.

Four persons shaking hands in crosswise fashion, foretell a coming marriage.

Two bells ringing in the house at one time foretell a parting. So also does a hollow cavity in a fresh-cut cake and a loaf that breaks in two while being cut.

To enter a house with the left foot first brings bad luck to the occupants." (p. 38.)

THE BOOK OF FORBIDDEN KNOWLEDGE
Johnson &co. 1910s

"List of Fortunate Hours (to be born)

January 2nd: From 30 minutes past 10 till 15 minutes past 11 in the morning; and from 15 minutes before 9 till 15 minutes before 11 at night.

15th: From 30 minutes past 9 till 15 minutes past 10 in the morning; and from 30 minutes past 7 till 15 minutes past 11 at night.

26th: From 30 minutes past 8 till 15 minutes past 9 in the morning; and from 7 till 15 minutes past 10 at night.

February 11th and 12th: From 30 minutes past 7 till 15 minutes past 8 in the morning; and from 15 minutes past 6 till 15 minutes before 9 at night.

21st: From 7 till 15 minutes before 8 in the morning, and from 15 minutes past 5 till 15 minutes before 8 at night.

25th and 26th: From 15 minutes before 7 till 30 minutes past 7 in morning; and from 15 minutes before 5 till 30 minutes past 7 in evening.

March 10th: From 5 till 15 minutes before 6 in the morning; and fromhorn 4 in the afternoon till 15 minutes before 7 in the evening.

April 6th: From 15 minutes past 4 till 5 in the morning; and from 30 minutes past 2 till 15 minutes past 5 in the afternoon.

20th: From 30 minutes past 3 till 15 minutes past 4 in the morning; and from 30 minutes past 1 till 15 minutes past 4 in the afternoon.

May 3rd: From 15 minutes before 3 till 30 minutes past 3 in the morning: and from 15 minutes before 1 till 30 minutes past 3 in the afternoon.

18th: From 2 till 15 minutes before 3 in the morning: and from 12 at noon till 15 minutes before 3 in the afternoon.

28th: From 15 minutes before 1 till 30 minutes past 2 in the morning; and from 15 minutes before 12 at noon till 30 minutes past 2 in the afternoon.

31st From 15 minutes before 1 till 30 minutes past 1 in the morning; and from 15 minutes past 10 in the morning till 15 minutes before 1 in the afternoon.

June 10th and 11th: From 15 minutes from 12 at night till 1 in the morning.

15th: From 10 in the morning till 2 in the afternoon; and from 15 minutes before 12 at night till 15 minutes before 1 in the morning.

25th: From 15 minutes past 9 in the morning till 12 at

noon; and from 11 to 12 at night.

29th: From 9 in the morning till 15 minutes before 12 at noon, and from 15 minutes before 11 till 15 minutes before 12 at night.

July 19[th:] From 15 minutes past 8 till 11 in the morning; and from 10 till 11 at night.

14th and 15th: From 8 till 11 in the morning; and from 10 till 11 at night.

28th: From 7 till 10 in the morning; and from 9 till 10 at night.

August 6th and 7th. From 30 minutes past 6 till 15 minutes past 9 in the morning; and from 15 minutes past till 15 minutes past 9 at night.

10th and 11th: From 15 minutes past 6 till 9 in the morning; and from 8 till 9 in the evening.

19th and 20th: From 30 minutes past 5 till 80 minutes past 8 in the morning; and from 30 minutes past 7 till 30 minutes past 8 in the evening.

25th. From 15 minutes past 5 till 8 in the morning; and from 7 till 8 in the evening.

September 4th: From 15 minutes before 5 till 30 minutes past 7 in the morning; and from 30 minutes past 6 till 30 minutes past 7 in the evening.

8[Th] and 9th: From 30 minutes past 4 till 15 minutes past 7 in the morning; and from 15 minutes past 6 till 15 minutes past 7 in the evening.

FOLK MAGIC, SUPERSTITION, AND CHARMS

17th and 18th: From 5 till 15 minutes before 5 in the morning; and from 15 minutes before 6 till 15 minutes before 7 in the evening.

23rd: From 30 minutes past 3 till 30 minutes past 5 in the morning; and from 30 minutes past 5 till 30 minutes past 6 in the evening.

October 3rd: From 3 till 15 minutes before 6 in the morning; and from 15 minutes past 4 till 15 minutes past 5 in the afternoon.

7th: From 15 minutes before 3 till 30 minutes past 5 in the morning; and from 30 minutes past 4 till 30 minutes past 5 in the afternoon.

16th: From 2 till 5 in the morning; and from 4 till 5 in the afternoon.

21st and 22nd: From 15 minutes before 2 till 30 minutes past 4 in the morning; and from 30 minutes past 3 till 15 minutes past 4 in the afternoon.

November 5th: From 1 till 15 minutes before 4 in the morning; and from 15 minutes before 3 till 15 minutes before 4 in the afternoon.

14th: From 15 minutes past 12 till 3 in the morning; and from 2 till 3 in the afternoon.

20th: From 15 minutes before 12 till 15 minutes past 2 in the morning; and from 15 minutes past 1 till 2 in the afternoon.

December 14th and 15th: From 10 till 30 minutes past 12 in the morning; and from 12 at noon till 15 minutes before 1 in the afternoon.

FOLK MAGIC, SUPERSTITION, AND CHARMS

18th and 19ᵗʰ: From 15 minutes before 10 at night till 15 minutes past 5 in the morning; and from 30 minutes past 11 till 15 minutes past 12 at night.

January 3ʳᵈ: From 30 minutes past 10 till 15 minutes past 11 in the morning; and from 15 minutes before 9 till 15 minutes past 11 at night.

12ᵗʰ and 13ᵗʰ: From 15 minutes past 9 till 10 in the morning; and from 15 minutes before 8 to 30 minutes past 10 at night.

18ᵗʰ: From 9 till 15 minutes before 10 in the morning; and from 15 minutes past 7 till 10 at night.

27ᵗʰ: From 9 till 15 minutes before 10 in the morning; and from 7 till 15 minutes before 10 at night.

February 1ˢᵗ: From 8 till 30 minutes past 8 in the morning; and from 6 till 30 minutes past 8 in the evening.

11ᵗʰ and 12ᵗʰ: From 15 minutes before 8 till 80 minutes past 8 in the morning; and from 15 minutes before 6 till 30 minutes past 8 in the evening.

17ᵗʰ: From 7 till 15 minutes before 8 in the morning; and from 15 minutes past 5 till 8 in the evening.

March 1ˢᵗ: From 30 minutes past 6 till 15 minutes past 7 in the morning: and from 30 minutes past 4 till 15 minutes past 7 in the evening.

16ᵗʰ and 17ᵗʰ: From 30 minutes past 5 till 15 minutes past 6 in the morning: and from 15 minutes before 4 till 30 minutes past 6 in the evening.

19ᵗʰ, 20ᵗʰ, 21ˢᵗ, 22ⁿᵈ, 23ʳᵈ, 24ᵗʰ, and 25ᵗʰ: From 30 minutes past 5 till 30 minutes past 6 in the morning: and from 30 minutes past 3 till 15 minutes past 6 in the evening.

26th, 27th, 28th, 29th, and 30th: From 15 minutes past 5 till 15 minutes before 6 in the morning: and from 15 minutes past 3 till 6 in the evening.

April 3rd, 4th, 5th, 6th, 7th, 8th, and 9th: From 30 minutes past 4 till 30 minutes past 5 in the morning; and from 30 minutes past 2 till 5 in the afternoon.

10th, 11th, 12th, 13th, and 14th: From 15 minutes before 4 till 15 minutes before 5 in the morning; and from 2 till 30 minutes past 4 in the afternoon.

19Th, 20th, 21st, 22nd, and 23rd: From 30 minutes past 4 in the morning; and from 15 minutes before 2 till 30 minutes past 4 in the afternoon.

25th, 26th, 27th, and 28th: From 3 till 4 in the morning; and from 15 minutes past 1 till 15 minutes before 4 in the afternoon.

May 3rd, 4th, 5th, 6th, 7th, and 8th: From 15 minutes past two till 15 minutes past 3 in the morning; and from 30 minutes past 12 at noon till 15 minutes past 3 in the afternoon.

9th,1, 10th, 11th, 12th, and 13th: From 2 till 3 in the morning; and from 15 minutes past 12 at noon till 3 in the afternoon.

16th, 17th, 18th, 19th, 20th, 21st, and 22nd: From 15 minutes before 2 till 15 minutes before 3 in the morning; and from 12 at noon till 15 minutes before 3 in the afternoon.

23Rd, 24th, 25th, 26th, and 27th: From 15 minutes past 1 till 15 minutes past 2 in the morning; and from 30 minutes past 11 in the forenoon till 15 minutes past 2 in the afternoon.

June 1st, 2nd, 3rd, 4th, .5th, and 6th: From 15 minutes past 10 in the morning till 1 in the afternoon: and from 15 minutes past 12 at night til 15 minutes past 1 the next morning.

11th: From 15 minutes past 10 in the morning till 15 minutes before 1 in the afternoon; and from 12 at night till 1 the next morning.

20th: From 30 minutes past 9 in the morning till 12 at noon; and from 11 till 12 at night.

25th: From 15 minutes past nine in the morning till 15 minutes past 12 at noon; and from 11 till 12 at night.

July 5th: From 15 minutes before 8 till 15 minutes past 10 in the morning; and from 15 minutes before 10 till 15 minutes before 11 at night.

9Th: From 15 minutes past 8 till 11 in the morning; and from 15 minutes past 10 until 11 at night.

19th: From 30 minutes past 7 till 10 in the morning; and from 15 minutes past 9 till 15 minutes past 10 at night.

24Th: From 7 till 15 minutes before 10 in the morning: and from 9 till 10 at night.

August 2nd and 3rd: From 30 minutes past 6 till 15 minutes before 9 in the morning; and from 30 minutes past 8 till 30 minutes past 9 at night.

6Th: From 15 minutes before 5 till 9 in the morning: and from 30 minutes past 7 till 30 minutes past 8 at night.

22nd: From 15 minutes past 5 till 8 in the morning; and

from 15 minutes past 7 till 15 minutes past 8 at night.

September 1ˢᵗ: From 4 till 15 minutes before 7 in the morning; and 6 till 7 in the evening.

5ᵗʰ: From 30 minutes past 4 till 15 minutes before 7 in the morning; and from 30 minutes past 6 till 30 minutes past 7 in the evening.

14ᵗʰ: From 15 minutes before 4 till 30 minutes past 6 in the morning; and from 30 minutes past 5 till 30 minutes past 6 in the evening.

29ᵗʰ: From 15 minutes before 3 till 30 minutes past 5 in the morning; and from 30 minutes past 4 till 30 minutes past 5 in the evening.

October 3ʳᵈ: From 3 till 15 minutes before 6 in the morning; and from 15 minutes before 5 till 15 minutes before 6 1n the evening.

12ᵀʰ: From 15 minutes past 3 till 5 in the morning; and from 15 minutes before 4 till 30 minutes past 4 in the afternoon.

18ᵗʰ and 19ᵗʰ: From 30 minutes past 1 till 4 in the morning; and from 15 minutes before 3 till 39 minutes past 4 in the afternoon.

November 10ᵗʰ and 11ᵗʰ: From 30 minutes past 12 at night till 15 minutes past 3 in the morning; and from 30 minutes past 1 till 30 minutes past 2 in the afternoon.

15ᵗʰ and 16ᵗʰ: From 12 at night till 15 minutes before 3 in the morning; and from 15 minutes past 1 till 2 in the afternoon.

29ᵗʰ and 30ᵗʰ: From 15 minutes past 11 at night till 2 in

the morning; and from 1 till 15 minutes before 2 in the afternoon.

December 8th and 9th: From 15 minutes past 10 at night till 1 in the morning; and from 30 minutes past 12 at noon till 30 minutes past 1 in the afternoon.

14[th,] 15th, and 16th: From 10 at night till 15 minutes before 11 in the morning; and from 15 minutes before 12 till 30 minutes past 12 at noon.

23rd and 24th: From 15 minutes past 11 til 12 at noon; and from 15 minutes past 9 till 12 at night.

28[th:] From 15 minutes past 10 till 11 in the morning; and from 9 till 15 minutes before 12 at night.

We do not presume to assert that every person born on the last mentioned times, will be exempt from all descriptions of trouble during the Whole of their lives, but that they will never (in spite of whatever may happen to befall them) sink below mediocrity. Even servants and those born of poor parents will possess some superior qualities; get into good company, much noticed by their superiors. And will, in spite of any intervening difficulties, establish themselves in the world and rise much above their sphere of birth.

It has often been recorded, and though a singular observation, experience has shown it to be a true one, that some event of importance is sure to happen to a woman in her thirty first year, whether single or married; it may prove for her good, or it may be some great evil or temptation; therefore we advise her to be cautious and circumspect in all her actions. If she is a maiden or Widow, it is probable she will marry this year. If a. Wife that she will lose her children or her husband. She will either receive riches or travel into a foreign land; at all events, some circumstance or other will take place during this remarkable year of her life, that will have great effect on her future fortunes and existence.

The like is applicable to men in their forty-second year, of which so many instances have been proved that there is not a doubt of its truth: Observe always to take a lease for an odd number of years; even are not prosperous- The three first days of the moon are the best for signing papers, and the first five days as well as the twenty fourth for any fresh undertaking. But we cannot but allow that a great deal depends on our own industry and perseverance, and by strictly discharging our duty to God and man, we may often overcome the malign influence of a bad planet, or a day marked as unlucky in the book of fate." (p. 16-26.)

FOLK CHARMS AND HEXES

CLAVICLES OF SOLOMON
Sloane (trans.) 17th Century

"To Cause a Thing to Appear Real though it Not Be Real

For such an experiment, you must write it on paper, as shall be hereafter appointed. Also you must write with blood, as shall be likewise declared with what blood; and what pen; if it is required that you should work this by writing, letters, or names, work as such chapters appoint you. This being done say with a low voice the following: Abac, Abdac, Istac, Castac, Adach, Castas, Calsac, Lusor, Triumphator, Derisor, Incantator. Be you here present at my work, and confirm it so as I desire, and make it so appear, that they that see it be deprived of their sight, and may see false things instead of true ones. Come all of you therefore to consecrate, and to enchant it, by Jesus of Nazareth, who has enjoined you to that office.

Which being done you may work with the forenamed names; Abac, Aldac, and so forth, and these are to be written in the end of your work, and if you work any other way, always observe that these words are to be said at the end of the same." (p. 29.)

EGYPTIAN SECRETS
L.W. DeLaurence 1900

"To Make Yourself Invisible

Pierce the right eye of a bat, and carry it with you, and you will be invisible." (p. 146.)

THE GRAND GRIMOIRE
18th Century

"To make Everything in an Apartment Appear Black:
Soak the wick of the lamp used to light the apartment in well beaten sea foam, adding to the lamp oil some sulfur and lead oxide in equal parts, and all those who enter the room will appear drunk and delirious." (p. 53-54.)

THE GREATER KEY OF SOLOMON
Samuel Mathers, 1914

"How to Render Oneself Invisible

Make a small image of yellow wax, in the form of a man, in the month January and in the day and hour of Saturn, and at that time write with a needle above the crown of its head and upon its skull which you shall have adroitly raised, the character following. (See Figure 5.) After which you shall replace the skull in proper position. you shall then write upon a small strip of the skin of a frog or toad which you shall have killed, the following words and characters. (See Figure 6.) You must then go and suspend the said figure by one of your hairs from the vault of a cavern at the hour of midnight, and burning temple incense under it, you shall say:

METATRON, MELEKH, BEROTH, NOTH, VENIBBETH, MACH, and all ye, I conjure thee oh Figure of wax, by the Living God, that by the virtue of these characters and words, thou render me invisible, wherever I may bear thee with me. Amen.

And after having burned temple incense again under it, you shall bury it in the same place in a small deal box, and every time that you desire to pass or enter into any place without being seen, you shall say these words, bearing the aforesaid figure in thy left pocket:

Come unto me and never quit me whithersoever I shall go.

Afterwards you shall take it carefully back unto the before-mentioned place and cover it with earth until you shall need it again." (p. 72-73.)

Note: Here follow figures 5 and 6 as referenced in the book:

POW WOWS
John George Hohman, 1822

"How to cause thieves to stand still without being able to move backwards or forwards

In using any prescription of this book in regard to making others stand still, it is best to be walking about; and repeat the following three times:

'Oh, Peter, oh Peter, borrow the power from God; what I shall bind with the bands of a Christian hand, shall be bound; all male and female thieves, be they great or small, young or old, shall be spell-bound, by the power of God, and not be able to walk forward or backward until I see them with my eyes, and give them leave with my tongue, except it be that they count for me all the stones that may be between heaven and earth, all rain-drops, all the leaves and all the grasses in the world. This I pray for the repentance of my enemies.' + + +

Repeat your articles of faith and the Lord's Prayer.

If the thieves are to remain alive, the sun dare not shine upon them before their release. There are two ways of releasing them, which will be particularly stated: The first is this, that you tell them, in the name of St. John, to leave; the other is as follows: 'The words which have bound thee shall give thee free.' + + +" (p. 35-36.)

"To Spellbind a Thief so that he Cannot Stir

This benediction must be spoken on a Thursday morning, before sunrise and in the open air:

'Thus shall rule it, God the Father, the Son, and the Holy Ghost. Amen. Thirty-three Angels speak to each other coming to administer in company with Mary. Then spoke dear Daniel, the holy one: Trust, my dear woman, I see some thieves coming who intend stealing your dear babe; this I cannot conceal from you. Then spake our dear Lady to Saint Peter; I have bound with a band, through Christ's hand; therefore, my thieves are bound even by the hand of Christ, if they wish to steal mine own, in the house, in the chest, upon the meadow or fields, in the woods, in the orchard, in the vineyard, or in the garden, or wherever they intend to steal. Our dear Lady said: Whoever chooses may steal; yet if anyone does steal, he shall stand like a buck, he shall stand like a stake, and shall count all the stones upon the earth, and all the stars in the heavens. Thus I give thee leave, and command every spirit to be master over every thief, by the guardianship of Saint Daniel, and by the burden of this world's goods. And the countenance shall be unto thee, that thou canst not move from the spot, as long as my tongue in the flesh shall not give thee leave. This I command thee by the Holy Virgin Mary, the Mother of God, by the power and might by which he has created heaven and earth, by the host of all the angels, and by all the saints of God the Father, the Son, and the Holy Ghost. Amen.'

If you wish to set the thief free, you must tell him to leave in the name of St. John.

Another way to bind thieves

'Ye thieves, I conjure you, to be obedient like Jesus Christ, who obeyed his Heavenly Father unto the cross, and to stand without moving out of my sight, in the name of the Trinity. I command you by the power of God and the incarnation of Jesus Christ, not to move out of my sight, + + + like Jesus Christ was standing on Jordan's stormy banks to be baptized by John. And furthermore, I conjure you, horse and rider, to stand still and not to move out of my sight, like Jesus Christ did stand when he was about to be nailed to the cross to release the fathers of the church from the bonds of hell. Ye thieves, I bind you with the same bonds with which Jesus our Lord has bound hell; and thus ye shall be bound; + + + and the same words that bind you shall also release you.'

To effect the same in less time

'Thou horseman and footman, you are coming under your hats; you are scattered! With the blood of Jesus Christ, with his five holy wounds, thy barrel, thy gun, and thy pistol are bound; saber, sword, and knife are enchanted and bound, in the name of God the Father, the Son, and the Holy Ghost. Amen.'

This must be spoken three times.

FOLK MAGIC, SUPERSTITION, AND CHARMS

To release spell-bound persons

'You horsemen and footmen, whom I here conjured at this time, you may pass on in the name of Jesus Christ, through the word of God and the will of Christ; ride ye on now and pass.'" (p. 60-62.)

THE BOOK OF FORBIDDEN KNOWLEDGE
Johnson &co 1910s

"That No Witch may Leave a Church

Purchase a pair of new shoes, grease them on Saturday with grease on the outer sole, then put them on and walk to the church, and no witch can find the way out of the church without you proceed before her." (p. 41.)

"To Obtain Money

Take the eggs of a swallow, boil them, return them to the nest, and if the old swallow brings a root to the nest, take it, put it into your purse, and carry it in your pocket, and be happy.

To Open Locks

Kill a green frog, expose it to the sun for three days. powder or pulverize it. A little of this powder put into a lock will open the same.

To Understand the Song of Birds

Take the tongue of a vulture, lay it for three days and three nights in honey, afterward under your tongue, and thus you will understand all the songs of birds." (p. 42.)

PROGNOSTICATION

EGYPTIAN SECRETS
L.W. DeLaurence 1900

"How a Farmer may be enabled to Predict the Future State of the Weather during the Year, from the first day of January, or from the Days of the First Week in which the Hew Year's Day Comes

If New-Year's Day falls upon a Sunday, a quiet and gloomy winter may be expected, followed by a stormy spring, a dry summer, and a rich vintage. When New-Year's Day comes on a Monday, a varied winter, good spring, dry summer, cloudy weather, and an inferior vintage may be expected. When New-Year's comes on a Wednesday, a hard, rough winter, a blustery, dreary spring, an agreeable summer, and a blessed vintage may be hoped for. If the first of the year happens to come on Thursday, a temperate winter, agreeable spring, a dry summer, and a very good vintage will follow. If on a Friday the year begins, a changeable, irregular winter, a fine spring, a dry and comfortable summer, and a rich harvest will be the result. If New-Year's Day comes on Saturday, a rough winter, bleak winds, a wet and dreary spring, and destruction of fruit will be the consequence." (p. 64.)

GRIMORIUM VERUM
18th Century

"Divination by the Egg:

The operation of the egg is to know what will happen to anyone who is present at such an experiment.

One takes the egg of a black hen, laid in the daytime, breaks it, and removes the germ from within. You must have a large glass, very thin and clear- fill this with clear water and into it put the egg germ. The glass is placed in the mid day in summer, and the director of the operation will recite the prayers and conjurations of the day.

These prayers and conjurations are such as are found in the *Key of Solomon* in which we treat amply of the airy spirits. And with the index finger, agitate the water, to make the germ turn, Leave it to rest a moment, and then look at it through the glass, not touching it. Then you will see the answer, and it should be tried on a work day, because there are spirits which will come during the times of ordinary occupations. If one wishes to see if a boy or a girl is a virgin, the germ will fall to the bottom. If he or she is not, it will be as usual." (p. 22.)

BIRDS IN LEGENDS, FABLES, AND FOLKLORE
Ernest Ingersoll, 1923

"The pagans of primitive times along the shores of the Mediterranean believed in personal gods and their guidance in human affairs. With the approval of these gods, or of that departmental god or goddess having charge of the matter in mind, one's project would prosper, whereas their disapproval meant failure and very likely some punishment under divine wrath. The human difficulty was to learn the will of said gods. Equally well settled was the doctrine that birds- which seemed to belong to the celestial spaces overhead where the gods lived and manifested their variable moods, now in sunshine and zephyr, now by storm-clouds, and rainfall- were inspired messengers of the gods, and required reverent attention.

This, however, did but throw the difficulty one step further back, for how could human intelligence comprehend the messages birds were constantly bringing? At any rate the principal and most numerous omens in the pre-Christian centuries were drawn from birds; and this kind of divination gained so much credit that other kinds were little regarded. It was based, as has been indicated, on the theory that these creatures, by their actions, wittingly or unwittingly, conveyed the will of the gods. This super-avian attribute was by no means confined to the prominent raven and crow, whose prophetic qualities have been portrayed in another chapter, for various birds came to be considered 'fortunate' or 'unfortunate,' from the point of view of the seeker after supernal guidance, either on account of their own characteristics or according to the place and manner of their appearance; hence the same species might, at different times, foretell contrary events. Let me quote here a succinct statement from The Encyclopedia Londonensis, published in the early part of the 18th century: 'If a flock of various birds came flying about any man it was an excellent omen. The eagle was particularly observed for drawing omens; when it was observed to be brisk and lively, and especially if, during its sportiveness, it flew from the right hand to the left, it was one of the best omens that the gods could give. Respecting vultures there are different opinions, both among the Greek and the Roman authors; by some they are represented as birds of lucky omen, while Aristotle and Pliny reckon them among the unlucky birds. If the hawk was seen seizing and devouring her prey, it portended death; but if the prey escaped deliverance from danger was portended. Swallows wherever and under whatever circumstances they were seen were unlucky birds; before the defeat of Pyrrhus and Antony they appeared on the tent of the former and the ship of the latter; and, by dispiriting their minds, probably prepared the way for their subsequent disasters. In every part of Greece except Athens, owls were regarded as unlucky birds; but at Athens, being sacred to Minerva, they were looked upon as omens of victory and success. The swan, being an omen of fair weather, was deemed a lucky bird by mariners.'

The most inauspicious omens were given by ravens, but the degree of misfortune which they were supposed to portend depended, in some measure, in their appearing on the right hand or the left; if they came croaking on the right hand it was a tolerably good omen; but if on the left a very bad one... The crow appearing (at a wedding) denoted long life to the married pair, if it appeared with its mate; but if it was seen single separation and sorrow were portended. Whence it was customary at nuptials for the maids to watch that none of these birds coming singly should disturb the solemnity. It was hardly to be expected that the comprehension of all this science of soothsaying should belong to ordinary mortals; and therefore there arose early in its development certain clever 'wise men' who declared themselves endowed with magical power to understand the language of birds, and to interpret both their chatter and their actions. Thus originated the profession of augury, a word that spells 'bird-talk' in its root-meaning, with its later product auspices, or 'birdviewers.'

The augur originally was a priest (or a magician, if you prefer that term) who listened to what the birds said; and the auspex was another who watched what they did, or examined their entrails to observe anything abnormal that he might construe as an answer to prayer, or interpreted something else in the nature of an omen from this or that divinity, or from all the gods together. I need not describe the elaborate rites and ceremonies that came to be associated with the practice of this kind of divination (ornithomancy), especially under the revered and powerful College of Augurs that practically ruled the Roman Republic, even in the Augustan age, for it will suffice to direct attention to a few features. Birds were distinguished by the Roman augurs as oscines or alites, 'talkers' and 'flyers.' The oscines were birds that gave signs by their cry as well as by flight, such as ravens, owls and crows. The alites included birds like eagles and vultures, which gave signs by their manner of flying. The quarter of the heavens in which they appeared, and their position relative to that of the observer, were most important factors in determining the significance of the supposed message, as has been extensively explained in an earlier chapter of this book." (p. 188-190.)

FOLK MAGIC, SUPERSTITION, AND CHARMS

ORIENTAL INTERPRETATION OF DREAMS
Barclay &Co, 1874

"The Art of Fortune Telling by the Nails of the Fingers

Black extremities of the nails: is a sign of husbandry.

Broad nails: show that the person is bashful and fearful, but of a gentle nature. When there is a certain white mark on the extremity of them, it shows that the person has more honesty that subtlety, and that his worldly substance will be impaired through negligence.

Fleshy nails: denote the person to be mild in temper, idle and lazy. Little and round nails: denote obstinate anger and hatred.

If they be crooked at the extremity, they show pride and fierceness.

Long nails: show the person to be good natured, but mistrustful, and loves reconciliation better than differences.

Narrow nails: denote the person to be inclined to mischief, and to do injury to his neighbor.

Oblique nails: signify deceit and want of courage.

Pale and black nails: show the person to be very deceitful to his neighbor, and subject to many diseases.

Red and marked nails: signify a choleric and martial nature, given to cruelty; and as many little marks as there are, they speak of so many evil desires.

Redness, of divers colors, at the beginning of the nails

shows the person to be choleric, and very quarrelsome.

Round nails: show a choleric person, yet soon reconciled, honest, and a lover of secret sciences.

White nails and long: denote much sickness and infirmity, especially fever, an indecision of strength and deceit by woman. If upon the white anything appears at the extremity that is pale, it denotes short life, by sudden death, and the person to be given to melancholy." (p. 172-173.)

"Charms to Know Who your Husband Will Be

1: This is to be attempted on the 21st of January, St. Agnes day. You must prepare yourself by a twenty-four hours fast, touching nothing bat pure spring water, beginning at midnight on the 20th, to the same again on the 21st; then go to bed, and pray to St. Agnes to let you see your husband, and you will dream of your future spouse: if you see more men than one in your dream, you will wed two or three times; but if you sleep and dream not, you will never marry.

2: A slice of the bridecake thrice drawn through the wedding-ring, and laid under the head of an unmarried woman, will make her dream of her future husband.

Christmas Spell

During Christmas week, steep mistletoe berries, to the number of nine, in a mixture of ale, wine, vinegar, and honey; take them oil going to bed, and you will dream of your future lot; a storm in this dream is very bad; it is most likely you will then marry a sailor, who will suffer shipwreck at sea; but to see either sun, moon or stars, it is an excellent presage; so are flowers; but a coffin is an index of a disappointment in love.

Lent Charm

To be tried on any Friday in Lent, Good Friday excepted, when it is improper to try any thing of the kind, and the mind ought to be more seriously disposed. Write twelve letters of the common alphabet on separate pieces of card; also twelve figures, and the same number of blank cards; then put them in a bag and shake them well, and let each present draw one; a blank shows a single life; a figure, intrigue in love concerns; and a letter a happy marriage.

Valentine Charm

If you receive one of those love tokens, and cannot guess at the party who sent it, or are in any doubt, the following method will explain it to a certainty: Prick the fourth finger of your left hand, and with a crow quill write on the back of the Valentine the day and hour in which you were born, and the date of the year; also of the present one, the moon's age, and the name of the present morning star, all of which you will find in the almanac, and the sign into which the sun has entered. Try this on the first Friday after you receive the Valentine, but do not go to bed till midnight; place the paper in your left shoe, and put it under your pillow. The young woman will be sure to dream of the identical person who sent the Valentine, and to see the man who is to be her husband.

The Love-Letter Charm

On receiving a love-letter that has any particular declaration in it, lay it wide open, then fold it in nine folds, pin it next to your heart, and thus wear it till bedtime, then place it in your left-hand glove, and lay it under your head. If you dream of gold, diamonds, or any other costly gem, your lover is true, and means what he says; if of white linen, you will lose him by death; and if of flowers, he will prove false. If you dream of his saluting you, he means not what he professes, and will draw you into a snare. If you dream of castles or a clear sky, there is no deceit, and you will prosper: trees in blossom show children; washing or graves shows you will lose your lover by death; and water shows that your lover is faithful, but that you will go through severe poverty with the party for some time, though all may end well." (p. 175-176.)

POPULAR HOME REMEDIES AND SUPERSTITIONS
OF THE PENNSYLVANIA GERMANS
A. Monroe Aurand Jr., 1941

"Weather Forecasting is Important

What, if anything; was more important to a farmer in the early days of our history, than an understanding of the probable state of the weather, not only for the morrow, but for a year or more in advance. Crops depended on favorable weather; they had to be rotated for successful farming. Most natural then, that we have our almanacs covering the weather forecast, signs of the zodiac, phases of the sun, moon and other planets; the religious and civil special days. Long range weather forecasts are said to be substantially as reliable over a period of time as the government forecast.

February 2 has been widely advertised as 'Ground-hog Day.' It has two other designations: 1. 'Woodchuck Day,' a better term than the former, (some say); and, 2. 'Candlemas'- an ecclesiastical festival held in honor of the presentation of the infant Christ in the temple and the purification of the Virgin Mary.

In Pennsylvania, particularly, the coming of 'Ground hog day' is looked forward to with some anticipation. When this little prophet appears from his "home," should he see his shadow, he returns promptly, and all the world may take due and timely notice that six weeks of winter will endure. (In some sections four weeks is the rule.) In many rural sections men of small stature are expected, or chided to remain indoors on this date if the weather is clear, so as not to unduly tempt the forces of nature which control the balance of winter. Generally animals of every sort and description may be used in foretelling the weather, being something man has had about him for centuries, observing their ways and habits. Animals used in forecasting include: The ass (four legged variety), beaver, bear, bull, cat, cattle, chipmunk, deer, dog, donkey, fox, ground-squirrel, goat, hog, horse, mole, mouse, muskrat, ox, rabbit, rat, sheep and wolf, etc.

Birds of all sorts, as well as trees, shrubs and grasses; even fish; also clouds, fog and frost; insects; the moon, sun and stars. We can foretell weather for all seasons of the year in many ways. For instance:

Cat- A cat lying on its side and turning its face upward foretells stormy weather.

Caterpillar- The color of the caterpillar foretells the severity of the winter; if the ends are black, the beginning and the end of winter will be hard; if the middle, then the middle of winter.

Chickens- If chickens molt on the forepart of the body first, then the early part of winter will be severe; if on the rear, then the end of winter.

Corn- Thick husk on corn foretells a hard winter; if the husk is so short that the ears protrude, the winter will be mild.

Corns- Aching corns are a sign of rain.

Days- As is the weather on the fifth day of the month, so it will be the rest of the month; as the last Friday, so the following month.

FOLK MAGIC, SUPERSTITION, AND CHARMS

Dog- A dog lying on its back indicates a change to stormy weather.

Food- If all the food on the table is eaten the saying is: 'Tomorrow will be a clear day.'

Goosebone- About the breastbone of a goose: When held up to the light, if it shows dark upon the whole rather than otherwise, we shall have a severe winter throughout; if mottled variable, the lighter aspects betokening snow; the darker, frosts. The general transparency of the bone denotes an open winter, the front part foretelling the state of that season before Christmas, and the inner part the weather after Christmas.

Lightning- Never point your finger at lightning.

Pain- Pain in a scar or in one's bones indicates rain, or an early change in the weather.

Rain- Morning showers and old women's dancing do not last long.

Snow- The number of snows during winter is indicated by the number of days from the first snow in fall to the next following full moon; or the first of the following month.

Sound- If a clock with brass works ticks very loud, or if you can hear trains, bells, or whistles at a great distance, or smoke hangs low, it is a sign of stormy weather.

Trees- If the tops of trees are bare while the sides are still covered with leaves, the winter will be mild; if the leaves fall first from the sides, the winter will be severe." (p. 26-29.)

SIGNS, OMENS, AND SUPERSTITIONS
Astra Cielo, 1918

"Stumbling and Falling

Falling has always been associated with the idea of evil, and its effects can only be averted by a quick-witted remark or a muttered invocation. When Caesar landed at Adrumetum in Africa, it is related that he tripped and fell upon his face. This was considered as an ill omen by his soldiers, but with great presence of mind he exclaimed: 'Thus do I take possession of thee, O Africa.' Thus he changed a sign of bad to one of good fortune. When William the Conqueror landed in England, he fell prone upon the ground. A great cry of despair went up from his army, but he raised himself smilingly and said: 'I have seized the country with both my hands.'

To fall while going upstairs is a sure sign that the victim will not marry within a year.

The falling of a picture from the wall is universally regarded as a bad omen and frequently foretells the death of the original of the picture in the case of a portrait.

It is related that a well-known English archbishop on entering his study one day, found his portrait lying on the floor, the cord that held it on the hook, having snapped. The sight so unnerved the prelate that he became ill, and died shortly after.

The Duke of Buckingham had a similar misadventure. On entering the council chamber, he found his portrait lying at full length on the floor. He died soon after.

A fall from a horse, besides being very inconvenient and often painful, is supposed to bring evil consequences. If two persons part on horseback, and one of them falls off his mount, the two will never meet again.

The fall of a window blind is accounted unlucky, but the evil can be averted by at once replacing it in its sockets.

The fall of a knife or fork to the floor is usually considered a good omen and foretells a visit from a friend; a female in the case of a knife, or a male in the case of a fork.

To fall downstairs is a very bad sign and signifies loss of health or money.

To stumble in the morning on coming downstairs is a sign of ill luck during the day.

A horse stumbling on the highway brings bad luck to his owner.

Stumbling at a grave is considered a bad omen.

Shakespeare says:

'How oft to-night
Have my old feet stumbled at graves!
For many men that stumble at the threshold
Are well foretold that danger lurks within.'

If you stumble over a stick or stone, turn back and kick it out of the way to avert trouble.

Cutting Hair and Nails

The paring of nails has given rise to some strange beliefs. So also has the cutting of hair. This is natural, as the clipping away of one's body is in itself uncanny and apt to give rise to superstitious conjectures.

FOLK MAGIC, SUPERSTITION, AND CHARMS

Sailors believe that to cut the nails or hair during a calm will provoke contrary winds. They, therefore, only cut them in a storm.

The ancients declared that nails and hair should not be pared or cut when in the presence of the gods, but in the secrecy of one's home.

Among the Arabians it is considered lucky to cut the nails and hair on Friday.

In some countries it is considered unlucky to cut a child's nails till it is a year old. They have to be bitten off.

In Scotland it is believed that if a child's nails are cut before it is a year old, it will grow up to be a thief. In other lands, it is thought the child will stammer.

The Jews burn their nail parings with a piece of wood, as a species of offering to insure good luck.

Personal Appearance

When a woman's eyebrows meet across her nose, it is a good sign. She will be happy whether she marries or not.

A woman whose hair grows down over her forehead in the shape of a peak, will never marry.

Clothes Superstitions

On rising in the morning, great care must be given to the way one dresses, as accidents often foretell trouble during the day. Augustus Caesar put on his left sandal awry and nearly lost his life in a mutiny.

A well-known writer says:

'Augustus by an oversight
Put on his left shoe before his right;
Had like to have been slain that day
By soldiers mutinying for pay.'

To put your shirt inside out is a good omen, providing you discover it in time and change it. If left on all day, beware of accidents.

To button your vest so that the buttons and holes come out uneven is a good sign.

It is well to put on the stocking of your right foot first and the shoe of your left foot.

To tear off a button while dressing is a bad sign. It should be remedied at once before going out of the house.

A hole in one's stocking is a good sign on the first day, but brings bad luck on the second.

To put the right shoe on the left foot or the reverse, is a sign of coming trouble.

To rip a garment the first time you put it on, is a bad sign.

To rend one's garments was in former days considered a symbol of mourning.

If you meet a person wearing new clothes, pinch him for good luck.

A proverbial saying when meeting a person with new clothes, is, 'May you have health to wear it, strength to tear it, and money to buy another.'

Coin given to a person wearing a new suit will bring him good fortune as long as the clothes last.

To put on a suit for the first time on Monday signifies that it will soon tear. You will have bad luck in wearing it.

Tuesday: Beware lest the suit catch fire. Keep out of speculation.

Wednesday: Things will go well with you. Your speculations will succeed.

Thursday: You will always appear neat and well dressed. You will make a good impression and get what you are after.

Friday: Not a good day to put on new attire. You will be successful only as long as the clothes remain fresh.

Saturday: Beware of catching cold. There is an element of bad luck in a new suit on this day.

Sunday: Happiness and good luck will follow him who puts on a new suit on the Sabbath.

On Arising

To get out of bed with the left foot is considered a forecast of bad luck. When a person is cross or irritable, we often say, 'He got out of bed with the wrong foot.'

To put your foot on a soft carpet or rug, on arising, foretells a successful day.

To stumble on getting up, is bad. You should go back to bed and try it again.

FOLK MAGIC, SUPERSTITION, AND CHARMS

To say 'Good luck' on arising, will insure success during the day.

It is considered unlucky to sing before breakfast. You may cry before supper.

It is unlucky to relate a bad dream before breakfast. It may come true.

To find a coin early in the morning is a sign for you to beware lest you lose money before the day is spent." (p. 63-68.)

STARS OF DESTINY
Trix Devos, 1922

"Influence of Ascending Signs

The following delineations of the effect of ascending signs are for the signs alone without any planet in the first house; if any planet be therein it will modify or accentuate these testimonies; if a fortunate planet, it will increase the good and diminish the adverse qualities, and vice versa if a malefic planet. Whatever sign is on the first house of your Horoscope that is your Ascending sign.

ARIES ASCENDING: They admire scientific thought and are quite philosophical; do not become discouraged easily, and they possess a sharp, penetrating will power. They are at their best when they can guide, control and govern themselves or others, as they have the ability to plan and map out the future and lay out modes of action. They are lovers of independence, fond of their own way and happy only in activity and command. The desire is to be at the head of things and leaders in thought and action. They are enterprising and ambitious, quite versatile, and usually rather headstrong and impulsive; forceful and determined in effort and expressive in speech; intense when interested, vehement when excited. Somewhat inclined to be fiery or quick tempered and ready to resent abuse or imposition and, while liable to go to extremes through indignation, they do not hold a grudge for any great length of time. They love justice and freedom; are enthusiastic admirers; have practical ideals, and possess an electric nature. The planetary significator is Mars.

TAURUS ASCENDING: Gives a self-reliant, persistent nature capable of working hard and long in order to accomplish their purposes. Gentle while unprovoked, but 'mad as a bull' when really angered, and, when opposed are stubborn and unyielding; are usually quiet and dogmatic and somewhat secretive or reserved concerning their affairs. They have a great deal of endurance, latent power and energy; are practical and organizing and usually sincere, reliable and trustworthy. They are fond of pleasure and love beauty in nature, art, music and literature, and are moved a great deal by feeling and sympathy. Possessing a magnetic quality, they are able to benefit those who are deficient in vitality or those who are irritable or nervous. They are careful and steady and able to carry to completion the projects which they undertake. They have the ability to earn money for others and are good at all executive work, matters connected with the earth and its products succeed under their supervision. The planetary significator is Venus.

GEMINI ASCENDING: Makes one ambitious, aspiring, curious and given to inquiry, investigation and experimenting; they are also apt, dexterous and active and capable of engaging in two or more pursuits at the same time. The nature is sympathetic and sensitive; the mind is intuitional, perceptive and imaginative, also quite idealistic and fond of all mental recreation. There is a liking for pleasure and for adventure and for science and educational pursuits. At times they are restless,anxious, high-strung and diffusive; mentally timid, indecisive, irritable and excitable. They love change and diversity and must be constantly busy to be happy, because inactivity causes them impatience. They have the ability to become very clever, as they are progressive, inventive, mechanical and ingenious. They possess inherent conversational and literary ability. They do best in occupations where there is a variety of employment, where the mind and hands can be engaged in several different things. The literary and educational world is their best outlet. The planetary significator is Mercury.

CANCER ASCENDING: Gives a changeable, sensitive and retiring disposition with many changes and ups and downs of position and occupation. They have a fertile imagination, are somewhat sentimental, sympathetic and talkative. They are fond of home and family; are industrious, frugal, economical and anxious to acquire the goods of life. Fear of ridicule or criticism makes them discreet, diplomatic and conventional. They appreciate approbation and are easily encouraged by kindness. They have a tenacious memory, especially for family or historical events. The emotions are strong and they delight in beautiful scenery and in romantic or strange experiences or adventures. They have psychic and mediumistic faculty, are very conscientious, receptive to new ideas, and have the ability to adapt themselves to environments. They are adapted to pursuits which embrace the catering for the masses and all matters of a fluctuating and public nature. The planetary significator is the Moon.

LEO ASCENDING: Gives a good-natured, philosophical, generous, kind-hearted, noble disposition. They are frank, free, outspoken, independent, impulsive, forceful and demonstrative in manner. Their nature is electric and inspiring. They have great hope, faith and fortitude, are energetic and lavish in the expenditure of energy and vitality when their sympathy or interest is aroused. In affection they are ardent, sincere and passionate. They are philanthropic, charitable, loyal, aspiring, conscientious, adaptable, inventive and intuitive; entertain high ideals; are imperious and fond of power and command; usually popular and leaders in their social sphere. They are generally good-tempered, though high strung and quick to anger, yet are very forgiving and do not hold a grudge for long. They receive and grant favors readily and are usually fortunate in the long run. They succeed best where they have authority to hold some high or responsible position in managing or executive departments. The significator is the Sun.

VIRGO ASCENDING: This makes one modest, conservative, thoughtful, contemplative and industrious. They have a desire for wealth, but require extra effort to save money; are very active, not easily contented, and learn readily and quickly; have good endurance and do not show their age. Mentally, they are very perceptive and somewhat intuitive; are of a speculative turn and often give way to worry and over-anxiety; are sensitive to surroundings and to the conditions of others. They are quite discriminating and careful of details. Cautious regarding their own interests and will not neglect the interests of others, being diplomatic, tactful and shrewd. They are prudent, economical and practical and usually act with forethought. They should always avoid drugs and animal foods and should study hygiene with regard to diet to obtain best health. Commercial and business affairs and matters connected with the earth and its products succeed under their careful supervision. The planetary significator is Mercury.

LIBRA ASCENDING: Gives keen sense of perception with foresight and good comparison. They love justice, order, peace and harmony, and are usually very courteous, pleasant and agreeable persons, and although quick in decision and anger, are easily appeased. They are fond of beauty in all forms, in nature, art, music, literature, etc., and can enter with zest into refined and cultivated pleasures and amusements and greatly enjoy the company and society of brave, happy, sunny and mirthful people. They are affectionate, sympathetic, kind, generous and compassionate; also idealistic, artisitc, adaptable, constructive, intuitive, impressionable and inspirational. They admire modesty and refinement; are ambitious and dislike unclean work and all discord. The best outlet for their talents is in the professions, and they have ability for lines requiring good taste, neat touch or fine finish. The planetary significator is Venus.

SCORPIO ASCENDING: Makes one reserved, tenacious, determined and secretive, possessing a quick, keen, shrewd, critical and penetrating mentality. They are somewhat inclined to be suspicious or skeptical and stingingly sarcastic. They are quick witted, quick in speech and action, and alert, forceful and positive. They are often blunt, brusque and seemingly fond of contest, but nevertheless they make strong and splendid friends. They possess grit and go-ahead-ativeness that will enable them to reach high attainments. They accomplish their purposes by subtlety, strength of will or by force if necessary. They have keen judgment and mechanical skill and much constructive or destructive ability. They enjoy travel, are fond of investigating mysteries and things occult; appreciating luxury, yet can be very frugal and economical. They are natural chemists, surgeons and contractors, and gifted in accomplishing things requiring muscular skill or aggressive enterprise. The planetary significator is Mars.

SAGITTARIUS ASCENDING: This gives a nature which is inclined to be jovial, bright, hopeful, generous and charitable. They love liberty and freedom, are very independent, dislike a master and will allow no one to order or drive them about, but are usually good-humored and honorable. In disposition they are frank, fearless, impulsive, demonstrative, outspoken, enterprising, nervously energetic, ambitious, sincere and quick to arrive at conclusions. They are sympathetic and loving, possess good calculation and foresight, are intuitive and prophetic, and, while often appearing blunt or abrupt; yet they rarely miss the mark in their deductions. At times they are restless, over-anxious and high-strung. They respect religious customs, enjoy outdoor sports, are fond of animals, and interested in travel, law, medicine and philosophy. In the professions or commercial world they are generally aggressive, progressive and aspiring; quick to see and take advantage of openings and to definitely consummate business arrangements. Always aim directly at the point in their affairs. The planetary significator is Jupiter.

CAPRICORN ASCENDING: Gives a serious, quiet, thoughtful, contemplative nature, possessing dignity and self esteem enough to look well after their interests. They are cautious, prudent, economical and practical, and usually act only after due premeditation. They are ambitious and persevering and can work hard and long without becoming discouraged. Capable of much endeavor where opportunity is afforded, especially in business; they possess organizing and concentrating ability, and, being determined and persistent, also having caution and calculation and deep thought, they can plan and carry out schemes of considerable magnitude. They are not demonstrative in feeling and do not readily show their sympathy, they prefer ideas to words and acts to promises. They are industrious, self reliant and thrifty; respect religion, are given to investigation, interested in theology and become very profound in any subject or science undertaken. If Saturn, the significator, is much afflicted in the horoscope, the native meets with many delays and disappointments, inclined to give way too readily to adverse circumstances and are restricted by poor health, otherwise they do well with matters connected with the Earth and its products, and with large corporations.

AQUARIUS ASCENDING: Gives a determined, quiet, patient, unobtrusive and faithful nature as a rule. They are philosophical in tone, very humanitarian and usually refined; fond of art, music, scenery and literature. In disposition are reasonable, thoughtful, discriminating, concentrative and intelligent. Everything in the mental world appeals to them and they are sincere, artistic and practical; fond of honor and dignity, active on reform, progressive in ideas, and possess a sympathetic, good-hearted, pleasant, generous nature. They are clear reasoners and very capable of dealing with facts. Have strong likes and dislikes, good memory and concentration; usually sociable and of large acquaintance. They are intuitive, fond of occult research, peculiar or eccentric in some ways. They succeed in pursuits where steady application of the mind and concentration of thought is necessary. They have inventive genius and literary ability. Uranus is the planetary significator.

PISCES ASCENDING: This gives a kind, loving, trustful, confiding, sympathetic nature. The disposition is industrious, courteous, affable, hospitable and methodical. They are idealistic, imaginative, impressionable, emotional, mediumistic, receptive and quiet. Apt in detail and orderly in manner. Quick to observe deficiencies in others or lack of completeness in anything. They are usually lacking in confidence and self-esteem, are modest and timid and hesitate about putting themselves forward. At times they are inclined to despondence, and become over-anxious, indecisive, and lacking in life and energy. Capable of developing fine psychometric, telepathic, intuitive and inspirational faculty. They love music, scenery and animals. They succeed in occupations that require industry, discretion and power to make the best of circumstances, and in any employment that brings some kind of change, or where attention to details and completeness is necessary. The planetary significator is Neptune." (p. 55-61.)

THE BOOK OF FORBIDDEN KNOWLEDGE
Johnson &co, 1910s

"The Witches Chain

Let three young women join together in making a long chain- about a yard will do- of Christmas juniper and mistletoe berries, and, at the end of every link, put an oak acorn. Exactly before midnight let them assemble in a room by themselves, where no one can disturb them; leave a window open, and take the key out of the keyhole and hang it over the chimney-piece; have a good fire, and place in the midst of it a long, thin log of wood, well sprinkled with oil, salt, and fresh mould; then wrap the chain round it each maiden having an equal share in the business; then sit down, and on your left knee let each fair one have a prayer book opened at the matrimonial service. Just as the last acorn is burned, the future husband will cross the room; each one will see her own proper spouse, but he will be invisible to the rest of the wakeful virgins. Those that are not be wed will see a coffin, or some misshapen form. Cross the room; go to bed instantly, and you will all have remarkable dreams. This must be done either on a Wednesday or Friday night, but no other.

Love's Cordial

(To be tried the third night of a new moon.)

Take brandy, rum, gin, wine, and the oil of amber, of each a teaspoonful, a tablespoonful of cream, and three of spring water; drink it as you get into bed Repeat:

'This mixture of love I take for my potion;
That I of my destiny may have a. notion;
Cupid befriend me, new moon be;
And show unto me that fate that's designed.'

You will dream of drink, and, according to the quality or manner of it being presented, you may tell the condition to which you will rise or fail by marriage. Water is poverty; and if you dream of a drunken man, it is ominous that you will have a drunken mate. If you dream of drinking too much you will fall, at a future period, into that sad error yourself, without great care; and what is a worse fright than an inebriated female? She cannot guard her own honor, ruins her own and family's substance, and often clothes herself with rage. Trouble is often used as an excuse for this vicious habit; but it gives more trouble than it takes away." (p. 10-11.)

ANIMAL FOLKLORE

ANCIENT CHARMS CURES AND USAGES OF IRELAND
Lady Wilde, 1890

"When changing your residence, it is unlucky to bring a cat with you, especially across a stream, and a red and white cat is particularly ominous and dangerous. If a black cat comes of her own accord to your house, keep her, she is a good spirit; but do not bring her, she must come freely, of her own good will. The tail of a black cat rubbed on the eyes has marvelous curative properties, and the blood of a black cat is largely used in all mystic cures for disease." (p. 55.)

"The cricket is looked upon as a most lucky inmate of a house, and woe to the person who may happen to kill one; for all the other crickets will meet in general assembly and eat up the offender's clothes, as a just retribution for the loss of a friend and relation. (p. 59.)

THE BOOK OF WEREWOLVES
Sabine Baring-Gould, 1865

"In Norway and Iceland certain men were said to be *eigi einhamir*, not of one skin, an idea which had its roots in paganism. The full form of this strange superstition was, that men could take upon them other bodies, and the natures of those beings whose bodies they assumed. The second adopted shape was called by the same name as the original shape, *hamr*, and the expression made use of to designate the transition from one body to another, was at *skipta homum*, or *at hamaz*; whilst the expedition made in the second form, was the hamfor. By this transfiguration extraordinary powers were acquired; the natural strength of the individual was doubled, or quadrupled; he acquired the strength of the beast in whose body he traveled, in addition to his own, and a man thus invigorated was called *hamrammr.*

The manner in which the change was effected, varied. At times, a dress of skin was cast over the body, and at once the transformation was complete; at others, the human body was deserted, and the soul entered the second form, leaving the first body in a cataleptic state, to all appearance dead. The second hamr was either borrowed or created for the purpose. There was yet a third manner of producing this effect-it was by incantation; but then the form of the individual remained unaltered, though the eyes of all beholders were charmed so that they could only perceive him under the selected form. Having assumed some bestial shape, the man who is *eigi einhammr* is only to be recognized by his eyes, which by no power can be changed. He then pursues his course, follows the instincts of the beast whose body he has taken, yet without quenching his own intelligence. He is able to do what the body of the animal can do, and do what he, as man, can do as well. He may fly or swim, if be is in the shape of bird or fish; if he has taken the form of a wolf, or if he goes on a *gandreio,* or wolf's ride, he is fall of the rage and malignity of the creatures whose powers and passions he has assumed." (p. 13-14.)

"In Norway it is believed that there are persons who can assume the form of a wolf or a bear (Huse-bjorn), and again resume their own; this property is either imparted to them by the Trollmen, or those possessing it are themselves Trolls. In a hamlet in the midst of a forest, there dwelt a cottager named Lasse, and his wife. One day he went out in the forest to fell a tree, but had forgot to cross himself and say his paternoster, so that some troll or wolf-switch (varga mor) obtained power over him and transformed him into a wolf. His wife mourned him for many years, but, one Christmas-eve, there came a beggar woman, very poor and ragged, to the door, and the good woman of the house took her in, fed her well, and entreated her kindly. At her departure the beggar woman said that the wife would probably see her husband again, as he was not dead, but was wandering in the forest as a wolf. Towards nightfall the wife went to her pantry to place in it a piece of meat for the morrow, when, on turning to go out, she perceived a wolf standing before her, raising itself with its paws on the pantry steps, regarding her with sorrowful and hungry looks. Seeing this she exclaimed, 'If I were sure that you were my own Lasse, I would give you a bit of meat.' At that instant the wolf skin fell off, and her husband stood before her in the clothes he wore on the unlucky morning when she had last beheld him." (p. 73-74.)

"According to a curious Lithuanian story related by Schleicher in his *Litauische Marchen*, a person who is a werewolf or bear has to remain kneeling in one spot for one hundred years before he can hope to obtain release from his bestial form. In the Netherlands they relate the following tale: A man had once gone out with his bow to attend a shooting match at Rousse, but when about half way to the place, he saw on a sudden, a large wolf spring from a thicket, and rush towards a young girl, who was sitting in a meadow by the roadside watching cows. The man did not long hesitate, but quickly drawing forth an arrow, took aim, and luckily hit the wolf in the right side, so that the arrow remained sticking in the wound, and the animal fled howling to the wood. On the following day he heard that a serving-man of the burgomaster's household lay at the point of death, in consequence of having been shot in the right side, on the preceding day. This so excited the archer's curiosity, that he went to the wounded man, and requested to see the arrow. He recognized it immediately as one of his own. Then, having desired all present to leave the room, he persuaded the man to confess that he was a were-wolf and that he had devoured little children. On the following day he died." (p. 77.)

THE CLAVICLES OF SOLOMON
Sloane (trans.) 17th Century

"Of the use of bat's blood

Take a bat, and exorcise her after this sort:

'Camac, Lamath, Omac, Cachac, Marbac, Glyac, Iamachar, Valmath, I adjure this bat, by the father, the son, and the holy ghost; and by all the words that ard spoken of him that you serve us: Oh you angel Adonay, Eloyt, and you angel Adonel, be you my aid and help, that I may accomplish my desire.'

Afterwards take the needle, and prick the bat under the right wing, and take her blood, and say:

'Oh almighty Adonay, Araton, Ossul, Heloy, Heloe, Helion, Essercon, Sadon, Deus, Deus, Infinitus, Jesus, Christus; be my helper, that this blood may have power in these my doings.'" (p. 47.)

DRAGONS AND DRAGON LORE
Robert Ingersoll, 1928

"In his narrative of his travels in Persia, published in London in 1821, Sir William Ouseley relates that in his time there stood near Shiraz the remains of a once mighty castle called Fahender after its builder, a son of the legendary king Ormuz (or Hormuz). This prince rebelled against his brother on the throne and took possession of Fars, with help from the Sassanian family, long before the founding of Shiraz in the 7th century A.D. The castle was repeatedly ruined and repaired as the centuries progressed, and local wiseacres maintain that in it are buried royal arms, treasures, and jewels hidden by the ancient kings, and these are guarded by a talisman. 'Tradition adds another guardian to the precious deposit- a dragon or winged serpent; this sits forever brooding over the treasures which it cannot enjoy; greedy of gold, like those famous griffins that contended with the ancient Arimaspians.'

This term 'Arimaspian' seems to have been a name among the more settled people of Persia for the more or less nomadic tribes of the plains and mountains west of them, who in subsequent times, nearer the beginning of our era, are seen following one another in great waves of conquering migration from the steadily drying pastures of what we now call Kurdistan westward to the steppes of southern Russia. The earliest of these known as a definite nation were the Cimmerians, who perhaps reached their special country north of the sea of Azov by migration across the mountains of Armenia and the Caucasus. These were followed and replaced by the Scythians, and they in turn were driven out or absorbed by the Sarmatians. The area they occupied successively north of the Black Sea has been explored by Russian archaeologists, who find that during several centuries previous to the Christian era a substantial though crude civilization existed there, and the worship, or at least a respect for, the snake-dragon prevailed among these peoples. The writings of Prof. M. Rostovtzeff make these investigations accessible to English readers. The dragon-relics discovered make it evident that the notions relating to this matter preserved among the barbarians and peasantry of north-central Europe, which we shall encounter later, were largely derived from these proto-Russians, especially the Sarmatians; and also that they influenced the ideas of the dragon that we shall find in China, with which these early people of the western plains were in constant communication by way of Turkestan, Tibet and Mongolia. Thus Osvald Siren, author of Chinese Art, in speaking of very early Chinese sculptures, and especially of dragon figures, remarks:

'It seems evident that these dragons are of Sarmatian origin. Their enormous heads and claws are sometimes translated into pure ornaments; their tails into rhythmic curves like the ornamental dragons on the runic stones in Gotland. These two great classes of ornamental dragons, the Chinese and the Scandinavian, are no doubt descendants from the same original stock, which may have had its first period of artistic procreation in western Asia. The artistic ideals of the northern Wei dynasty remained preponderant in Chinese sculpture up to the sixth century (A.D.).'" (p. 29-30.)

"The dragon possesses the power of self-transformation, may make itself dark or luminous, or render itself invisible. A Chinese informed Mr. Ball that it becomes at will reduced to the size of a silkworm, or swollen till it fills the space of heaven and earth. When its breath escapes it forms clouds, sometimes changing into rain at other times into fire; and its voice is like the jingling of copper coins. Formerly, glass was thought to be its solidified breath. The creature may descend into the depths of the ocean, and rest in palaces of pearl. In early days, if ancient books are trustworthy, there were tame dragons- they dragged the chariots of legendary kings; and Visser found a tradition of a family making it their business to breed them for the emperors- hence their family name Hwan-lung, 'dragon-rearer.' Later it became the custom to ornament the prows of pleasure-junks with dragon-heads, and certain kinds of long, slender boats are known as 'dragon-boats' to this day. A popular story relates the adventures of a sort of celestial Robin Hood, Feng Afoo-chow, who stole from the rich and gave to the poor. He rode about the country on a winged, fire-breathing dragon (precursor of the automobile?), righted wrongs and appropriated treasure, until at last he perpetrated a theft of such magnificence that he left it to be the crown of his career, and settled down to remain a law-abiding citizen until his tame dragon bore him to the heaven of the repentant rich.

The popular understanding is that dragons were supernaturally created but are of different sexes, and are able to reproduce their kind; and according to Visser the book Pei Ya supports the general opinion that they are born from eggs. When these are about to hatch the sound made by a male embryo makes the wind rise, whereas the cry of a female 'chick' causes the wind to abate and change its direction. One account of how the sexes differ explains that the male dragon's horn is 'undulating, concave and steep'; it is strong on the top but very thin below. The female has a straight snout, a round mane, thin scales and a stout tall. Dragons' eggs are the beautiful pebbles picked up beside mountain brooks; and they are preserved by nature until they split in a thunderstorm, releasing a young dragon which immediately goes up to the sky. An old woman who found such eggs had various adventures with them that children like to hear about. A dragon's egg much bigger than a hen's egg, light and apparently hollow, was found, history says, in the Great River in the tenth century; and to it, in the opinion of the local people, was due subsequent calamitous floods. Another egg found was very heavy, and when shaken rattled as if it contained water; perhaps it was a geode- at any rate it became an object of worship.

An interesting legend is appropriate here. The uppermost and worst cataract in the Yangtse gorges, known as the New or Glorious Rapid, was formed in 1896 by a landslip that filled three-fourths of the channel. The rivermen account for this mishap thus, as related by Dingle: 'The ova of a dragon being deposited in the bowels of the earth at this particular spot in due course of time hatched out... The baby dragon grew and grew, but remained in a dormant state until quite full-grown, when, as the habit of the dragon is, it became active, and at the first awakening shook down the hillside by a mighty effort, freed itself from the bowels of the earth, and made its way down to the sea.' A ford in the upper Hoang Ho is called Dragon-Gate. Fishes that pass above it become 'dragons'; those that fail remain simple fishes. Rapids and waterfalls in various parts of the country, and in Japan, have the same name and frequently a similar story." (p. 58-60.)

EGYPTIAN SECRETS
L.W DeLaurence 1900

" That no Ill may befall the Cattle

Whenever you bake, you should give them the slake water to drink, and naught will happen to them." (p. 18.)

"When Cattle is Bewitched

Take witchcraft balsam, glow worm oil, black juniper berry, oil of rue, oil of turpentine, two cents worth of each. Give this mixture to the cattle; also, some balsam of sulfur." (p. 19.)

"When the Udder of a Cow is Bewitched

Take blue bottle flowers, of which make a wreath; milk every stroke back of the legs three times upon the wreath; after this let the cow eat that wreath, and speak the following words: cow, I here give you bottle flowers that thou wouldst give me milk at once, that will not sour. Furthermore, whenever the cattle is driven out for the first time, in early spring, give to every piece of cattle a piece of beef meat about a half a finger long. This push down their throat after sprinkling it with a little salt." (p. 22.)

"How to drive away Bed Bugs

Fern leaves gathered between the last two days of the month of June, and put under the bed, will drive away the bed bugs sure." (p. 36.)

"To Prevent Bees from Flying Away

Take the root of a blue lily, put it into the bee hive. Probatum." (p. 158.)

FISHES FLOWERS AND FIRE
Hargrave(?) 1890

"'Fish' says Moule, 'have often been made the vehicle of religious instruction, and for this purpose all the fine arts have been put in requisition. among many pictures by the first masters in which the finny tribe are introduced, that of Saint Anthony, of Padua, preaching to the fish, may be mentioned. This fine picture, by Salvator Rosa, is in the collection at Ilthorp House, in Northamptonshire; the sermon itself is given in Addison's Travels in Italy. On the conventual seal of Glastonbury Abbey are represented the figures of Saint Dunstan between Saint Patrick and Saint Benignus; each has his emblem beneath his feet; the last has a party of fish- perhaps, adds the historian of the abbey, he also preached to them, as Saint Anthony did. A fish furnishing the University of Cambridge with a religious feast was the occasion of a tract, entitled 'Vox Piscis; or, the Book-fish;' containing three treatises which were found inside a cod fish in Cambridge market, on Midsummer Eve, 1676. This fish is said to have been taken in Lynn deeps, and after finding a book within it, the fish was carried by the bedel to the vice-chancellor, and coming as it did at the commencement, the very time when good learning and good cheer were most expected, it was quaintly remarked, that this sea guest had brought his book and his carcass to furnish both.'" (p. 9-10.)

"Ptolemus says that Ceres was called Sito among the Syracusans, from the same Greek word Sito. But he is mistaken, for, while he derives it from Dagon (which means fruit), he should have deduced it from Dag (which means a fish). There is the most ancient testimony outside of the Bible in regard to this god of Asia in what Berosus, Apollodorus, and Polyhistor write concerning Oannes. Por Oannes is mentioned as a two-headed animal; that feet like those of human beings grew from his tail, and that the rest of him is a fish. His voice was likewise human, and they say that, emerging from the Red Sea, he came to Babylon, but that he returned to the sea at sunset. He did this every day as if he were an amphibious animal, Prom him men learned all the various arts, letters, agriculture, the consecration of temples, architecture, political government, and whatever could possibly pertain to civilized life, and the most wonderful history of Belus and Omorea. His image was preserved down to the time of Berosus, that is, to the beginning of the Grecian monarchy. This marine god can be no other than Dagon, whose history is found in Samuel.

He was worshiped not only by the Philistines, but by the Babylonians also. Apollodorus, from the same Berosus, narrates more extensively of four Oannes, called Annedotos, who likewise in the lapse of ages appeared out of the Red Sea, every one of whom was half man and half fish. But in the time of Aedoracus, king of the Chaldeans, who preceded the deluge a few ages, another similar figure appeared, who was called Odakon. Dagon is undoubtedly intended and referred to in this fable of Odakon. Abydenos speaks of a second Annedotos, and bestows on him the form of a semi-demon. Helladius Besantinus speaks of a certain man of the name of Oleus arising out of the Red Sea, whose head, hands and feet were human, but that the other members of the body were those of a fish and that he taught letters, and the science of astronomy. As all these references are so applicable to the Oannes of Besorus, it is more than probable that the librarian made the mistake in the name of abbreviation in the copy." (p. 21-22.)

THE GRAND GRIMOIRE
18th Century

"The Secret of the Black Hen:

The famous secret of the Black Hen, a secret without which one can not count on the success of any Kabbala, was lost for a long time: after much investigation we have succeeded in finding it and the tests which we have carried out, to assure ourselves that it was positively that which we sought, exactly matched our expectations. Therefore we are completely satisfied. It is to share our happiness with all those who have the courage to imitate us that we have transcribed it. Take a Black Hen that has never been laid eggs and that has never been approached by a rooster and in taking her make certain that she does not cry out so that you will have to do this at eleven at night, when she is sleeping. Take her neck and close her throat so that she can not scream. Then go where two streets form a cross and at midnight precisely make a circle with a cyprus branch, go into the middle of the circle and cut the hen's body into two parts uttering the following words three times: ELOHIM, ESSAIM, search and then turn your gaze toward the East, kneel and recite the prayer." (p. 48-49.)

Note: this particular entry is from the initially Italian version and appears to have been pegged on to the initial content which was largely about summoning.

BIRDS IN LEGENDS, FABLES, AND FOLKLORE
Ernest Ingersoll, 1923

"Again, there is the story of the miraculous dove at the consecration of Clovis on Christmas Day, 496, at Rheims. When Clovis and St. Remi, the bishop, reached the baptistery the priest bearing the holy chrism was prevented by the density of the crowd from reaching the font. Then a dove, whiter than snow, brought a vial (ampoule) filled with chrism sent from heaven; and the bishop took it, and with this miraculous chrism perfumed the baptismal water for the Frankish chief by whose victories over Germanic barbarians France was founded. The lives of medieval saints and martyrs- or at any rate, the records of them- abound in such incidents of supernatural recognition. Several devoted women on taking the vow of virginity received their veils from doves hatched in no earthly nest; bishops were more than once given approval of public acts, especially when unpopular, by similar manifestations of divine approbation, doves alighting on their heads. 'A dove is the special emblem of Gregory the Great (A. D. 590-604), and its figure rests on his right shoulder in the magnificent statue of this pope in Rome.' This is in allusion, according to The Catholic Encyclopedia, 'to the well-known story recorded by Peter the Deacon (Vita, xxviii), who tells us that when the pope was dictating his homilies in Ezechiel a veil was drawn between his secretary and himself. As, however, the pope remained silent for long periods of time, the servant made a hole in the curtain and, looking through, beheld a dove seated on Gregory's head with its beak between his lips. When the dove withdrew its beak the holy pontiff spoke and the secretary took down his words; but when he became silent the servant again applied his eyes to the hole and saw that the dove had again placed its beak between his lips.' Much the same incident belongs to the biography of another early pope; and apropos to the significance of this bird in the Romanist method of demonstrating that faith to the populace, Mackenzie E. Walcott contributed the following bit of history to *Notes and Queries* in 1873:

'The dove was regarded as the symbol of the holy spirit which came in the eventide of days, bringing safety and peace to the ark of Christ and a world rescued from wreck, and to whom Christians should be conformed in innocence. A dove was suspended over the altar, as Amphilochius says of S. Basil that he broke the Holy Bread and placed one third part in the pendant golden dove over the altar. The Council of Constantinople charged a heretic with robbing the gold and silver doves that hung above the fonts and altars. The dove was also the symbol of our Blessed Lord, as we learn from Prudentius and an expression of Tertullian, 'the Dove's house,' applied to a church, probably in allusion to Coloss. I, 20. The dove for reservation (that is, withholding a part of the eucharist) whether for communion of infants in the baptistery, or of sick under a ciborium, was suspended by a chain. One is preserved in the church of S. Nazarius at Milan, and a solitary mention of another is contained in an inventory of Salisbury. In Italy at an early date, the dove was set upon a tower for reservation... We also find in early works of devotional art the dove represented as flooding a cross with streams of living water. There is a famous example in the Lateran, symbolical of Holy Baptism. A holy lamb and dove are placed on the canopy of the baptistery at Saragossa.'

It seems unlikely that Mohammed could have heard of these pontifical sources or methods of divine inspiration, yet, according to Brewer, (34) Prideaux, in his *Life of Mahomet,* relates that he taught a dove to pick seed placed in his ear as it perched on his shoulder; but the wily prophet 'gave it out it was the Holy Ghost, in the form of a dove, come to impart to him the counsels of God.' This accounts probably (for Shakespeare may well have heard the tradition) for the doubting query in Henry V: 'Was Mohammed inspired with a dove?'

Whether this legend is credible or not, it is certain that Islam has preserved the ancient Oriental reverence for this bird, which now flocks in great numbers around all the mosques; and the Moslems have a half-superstitious feeling that any bird that seeks its rest and makes its nest about temples and holy buildings must not be disturbed- a kindly regard in which swallows share, at least in the Near East, where the Mohammedans say that the swallow must be a very holy bird, because it makes an annual pilgrimage to Mecca. John Keane, an Englishman who spent a long time in Arabia about forty years ago, records that at Mecca vast flocks of pigeons were to be seen in the public space surrounding the Kaaba. By repeated observations he estimated that between 5,000 and 6,000 pigeons assembled there daily, all so tame that they would alight on men's heads and shoulders. They are still held as almost sacred, are never killed, and nest in nearly every building in niches left for that purpose in the walls of the rooms. Pilgrims purchase baskets of grain to give to the pigeons as a pious act, and each benefactor 'becomes the vortex of a revolving storm of pigeons.'

In some remote places, indeed, these temple-pets become themselves almost objects of worship. For example, on the direct road between Yarkand and Khotan, Chinese Turkestan, stands the locally celebrated pigeon-shrine (Kaptar Mazzar), where all good Moslems must dismount and reverently approach the sacred spot. 'Legend has it that Imam Shakir Padshah, trying to convert the Buddhist inhabitants of the country to Islam by the drastic agency of the sword, fell here in battle against the army of Khotan, and was buried in the little cemetery. It is affirmed that two doves flew forth from the heart of the dead saint, and became the ancestors of the swarms of pigeons we saw... sated with the offerings of the Faithful, and extremely fat... We were told that if a hawk were to venture to attack them it would fall down dead.'" (p. 120-123.)

"'The crow and the raven,' MacBain announces, 'are constantly connected in the Northern mythologies with battle-deities. 'How is it with you, Ravens?' says the Norse Raven Song. 'Whence are you come with gory beak at the dawning of the day... You lodged last night, I ween, where ye knew the corses were lying.' The ravens also assist and protect heroes both in Irish and Norse myth. It was a lucky sign if a raven followed a warrior.'

But the bold Norse sailors made a more practical use also of this knowing bird, for in those days, before the compass, they used to take ravens with them in their adventurous voyages on the fog-bound northern seas, and trust the birds to show them the way back to land. A notable instance was Floki's voyage to Iceland in 864 A. D., a few years after that island's discovery; and the French historian Mallet narrates it thus: We are told that Floki, previous to setting out on his expedition, performed a great sacrifice, and having consecrated three ravens to the gods took them with him to guide him on his voyage. After touching at the Shetland and Faroe islands he steered northwest, and when he was fairly out at sea, let loose one of his ravens, which, after rising to a considerable elevation, directed its flight to the land they had quitted... The second bird, after being some time on the wing, returned to the ship, a sign that the land was too far distant to be descried even by a raven hovering in the sky. Floki therefore continued his course, and shortly afterwards let loose his third raven, which he followed in its flight until he reached the eastern coast of Iceland. This is a somewhat poetic account, I imagine, of what perhaps was a more prosaic custom of seamanship, for doubtless it was usual at that time to carry several birds on such voyages, and to let them fly from time to time that they might learn and indicate to the voyagers whether land was near, and in what direction, as did old Captain Noah, master of the good ship Ark. Berthold Lauffer treats of this point with his customary thoroughness in his pamphlet Bird Divination:

Indian Hindu navigators kept birds on board ship for the purpose of dispatching them in search of land. In the Baveru-Jataka it is 'a crow serving to direct navigators in the four quarters'... Pliny relates that the seafarers of Taprobane (Ceylon) did not observe the stars for the purpose of navigation, but carried birds out to sea, which they sent off from time to time and then followed the course of the birds' flying in the direction of the land. The connection of this practice with that described in the Babylonian and Hebraic traditions of the deluge was long ago recognized... When the people of Thera, an island in the Aegean Sea emigrated to Libya, ravens flew along with them ahead of the ships to show the way. According to Justin... it was by the flight of birds that the Gauls who invaded Illyricum were guided. Emperor Jimmu of Japan (7th century) engaged in a war expedition and marched under the guidance of a gold-colored raven. Mr. Lauffer might have added that Callisthenes relates that two heaven-sent ravens led the expedition of Alexander across the trackless desert from the Mediterranean coast to the oasis of Ammon (Siwah), recalling stragglers now and then by hoarse croaking.'

The folklore of northern Europe is full of the cunning

and exploits of this bird and its congeners, which it would be a weary task to disentangle from pure myth. In Germany there is, or was, a stone gibbet called, with gruesome memories, Ravenstone, to which Byron alludes in Werner:

> 'Do you think
> I'll honor you so much as save your throat
> From the Ravenstone by choking myself?'

We read that the old Welsh king Owein, son of Urien, had in his army three hundred doughty ravens, constituting an irresistible force; perhaps they were only human "shock" troops who bore this device on their targes. Cuchulain, the savage hero of Irish fables, had, like Odin, two magic ravens that advised him of the approach of foes. Old-fashioned Germans believe that Frederick I (Barbarossa) is sleeping under Raven's Hill at Kaiserlauten, ready to come forth in the last emergency of his country. There in his grotto-palace a shepherd found him sleeping. Barbarossa awoke and asked: 'Are the ravens still flying around the hill?' The shepherd answered that they were. 'Then,' sighed the king, 'I must sleep another hundred years.'" (p. 143-146.)

"The little Grecian owl- it is a foreign replica of our own small screech owl, which, as a matter of fact, gurgles rather melodiously instead of screeching- was well thought of in Athens in its prime, and was the special cognizance of the wise and dignified goddess of her citizens, Pallas Athene- Minerva of the Romans. De Kay, indeed, reasons her out an owl-goddess, and it is said that statues of her have been found with an owl's instead of a human head. If she was a humanized expression for the moon, as some interpret her, this little lover of moonlight is most suitable as her symbol. Therefore one need not speculate on the reputed 'wisdom' of the owl, any owl- said to be proved wise by its being the only bird that looks straight before it- for that reputation is merely a reflection from the attributes of its patron, the stately goddess. Homer makes Athene the special protector of those, chiefly women, engaged in textile crafts; and there is an old saying that the owl was a weaver's daughter, spinning with silver threads. When, therefore, in the midst of the momentous naval battle of Salamis an owl alighted on the mast of the flagship of Admiral Themistocles, as tradition attests, it was received as an assurance from Pallas Athene herself that she was fighting with and for the harassed Greeks.

The bird is displayed as large as space permits on Greek coins of the period. When the Romans took over Athene as Minerva her owl came with her, but its symbolic importance quickly faded. The Italians cared nothing for their little 'strix' had no use for it except to eat it or make it a lure for their bird-catching nets, and even charged it with sucking the blood of children; and they had no respect at all for the rest of its tribe. The language applied to them by the Latin poets reveals the detestation and dread with which owls were held among the Romans. Derogatory references abound in books of the classical era, and similar sentiments might be quoted from authors down into medieval times. Even the elder Pliny, called a naturalist, but really hardly more than a too credulous compiler, condemns the tribe in very harsh words- especially the big-horned species; yet he only reflected the general belief that they were messengers of death, whence everybody trembled if one was seen in the town or alighted on any housetop. One luckless owl that made a flying trip to the Capitol was caught and burnt, and its ashes were cast into the Tiber. Twice Rome underwent ceremonial purification on this account, whence Butler's jibe in *Hudibras*:

'The Roman senate, when within
The city walls an owl was seen,
Did cause their clergy with lustrations
(Our synod calls humiliations)
The round-faced prodigy t' avert
From doing town and country hurt.'

The deaths of several Roman emperors, among them

Valentinian and Commodus Antoninus, were presaged by owls alighting on their residences, and it is recorded that before the death of the great Augustus an owl sang on the Curia. In central India the owl is now generally regarded as a bird of ill omen. 'If one happens to perch on the house of a native, it is a sign that one of his household will die, or some other misfortune befall him within a year. This can only be averted by giving the house or its value in money to the Brahmins, or making extraordinary peace-offering to the gods.' It is easy to calculate the origin of that particular form of superstition. In southern India, according to Thurston (quoted by Lauffer), the same dread prevails; and there the natives interpret the bird's cries by their number, much as they did those of crows. 'One such screech forebodes death; two screeches, success in any approaching undertaking; three, the addition by marriage of a girl to the family; four, a disturbance; five, that the hearer will travel. Six screeches foretell the coming of guests; seven, mental distress; eight, sudden death; and nine signify favorable results. The number nine plays a great role in systems of divination.'" (p. 160-162.)

"But of all the fabulous birds that infest ancient Persian mythology none is held so important as the falcon-like 'karshipta,' which brought the sacred law into the Paradise of Jamshid. 'Regarding the karshipta they say that it knew how to speak words, and brought the religion to the enclosure which Yim made, and circulated it: there they utter the Avesta in the language of birds.' We read also of a gigantic bird in Iran, the 'kamar,' 'which overshadowed the earth and kept off the rain till the rivers dried up.' In the Hindu mythology Vishnu is the sun-god, while Indra represents the lightning and storm, and the two are in general opposites, rivals, enemies. Vishnu rides on an eagle of supernatural size and power called garuda. In the Pahlavi translation of the stories the simurgh takes the place of the eagle, for their characters as well as their names are interchangeable. Garuda was born from an egg laid by Vinata, herself the daughter of a hawk and the mother of the two immense vultures that in Persian myths guard the gates of hell, and elsewhere figure boldly in Oriental fables; it is a mortal enemy, now of the serpent and now of the elephant, and now of the tortoise- all three connected with Indra. This bird carries into the air an elephant and a tortoise in order to devour them, and in one of the various accounts leaves them on a mountain-top as did the simurgh and the rukh their iniquitous 'liftings.' Garuda also appears in Japanese legendary art as gario, or binga, or bingacho, or karobinga, half woman, half bird, a sort of winged and feathered angel with a tail like a phenix and legs like a crane. This reminds us of the harpies of Greece. The Malays recognize the image, and when a cloud obscures the sun Perak men will say: 'Gerda is spreading his wings to dry.'

The Chinese, and after them the Japanese, had a phenix-like bird in their mythical aviary, which persists in the faith of the more simple-minded of their peoples, and as a fruitful motive in the decorative art of each. It was one of the four supernatural creatures that in ancient Chinese philosophy symbolized the four quarters of the heavens. The Taoists, whose religious ideas are older than Confucianism and prevailed especially among the humble and unlearned, called it the Scarlet Bird, and associated it with the element Fire, and with their mystic number 7. Archaic pictures show a crested bird with long tail-feathers- a figure that might well be meant for a peacock. The creature itself is said not to have been seen by mortal eyes since the time of Confucius, but it has by no means been forgotten, for it is the fungwhang, or feng-huang (which is the names of the male and the female of the species conjoined); and it lives even now on embroidered screens and painted vases, or proudly distinguishes royal robes, from the Tibetan mountains to the Yellow Sea." (p. 183-184.)

THE LORE OF THE UNICORN
Odell Shepard, 1930

"The unicorn has a less prominent role in the romances of the Middle Ages than one might expect, considering his potentialities, but this fact merely reminds one again that he was not regarded as exceptionally romantic or wonderful. The title of Le Romans de la Dame a la Lycorne et du Biau Chevalier au Lyon arouses expectations which are not fulfilled, for here the animal's function is largely symbolic. He is given to the heroine by Li Diex d'Amours in recognition of her tres grant purte, and all that he has to do in the course of eighty-five hundred lines is to swim the moat surrounding the Castle of Chief d'Or with his mistress on his back- the lion belonging to the hero, similarly mounted, paddling proudly beside him. Far more interesting than this merely ornamental beast is the unicorn we meet towards the end of the charming Old French prose romance called *Le Chevalier du Papegau*. King Arthur, wandering on his maiden adventure, has been stranded on a strange coast, and there he finds a square red tower, without door or window, in which a dwarf is living. The dwarf tells Arthur that he and his wife had been set on shore there many years before by the Lord of Northumbria, and that his wife had died shortly after giving birth to a son. 'When my wife was dead and I had buried her,' says he, 'I put my food into my overcoat, wrapped up my child as best I could, and then went through the forest looking for a hollow tree where I might rest and find shelter from the rain and the night and the wild beasts. At last I found one with a hollow large enough for six knights to lie in, and within the hollow there were newborn fawns, each one with a little horn in the middle of its brow. And when I saw these fawns I went inside and looked at them for a long time with wonder, and I sat down among them. While I was sitting there the mother came- a huge beast, as large as a large horse, with a horn in her brow as sharp as any razor in the world and with fourteen great udders of which the smallest was as large as the bag of a cow, and when this beast saw me she looked at me so terribly that I leaped up and dropped my child and fled. The child began to cry bitterly- and you are to know that it was the finest and fairest infant that ever was seen- so that the beast was touched with pity and she came into the hollow, while I lay hidden behind a root looking to see what she would do to the child. She lay down before him and put the nipple of her udder in his mouth and nursed him until he fell asleep. All that night I lay there without sleep and without daring to move for fear that the beast might kill me, and the child lay sleeping among the fawns. In the morning the unicorn went out to feed and I arose and took up the child, but while I was swaddling him she returned again. This time, however, she showed me such affection that I stayed with her; and when my son and the fawns had been suckled, the beast, who saw that I was little- for I am a dwarf- seemed to think that I must be young, and she made a motion with her head toward one of her udders that was still quite full. Being very thirsty, I did as she wished, and I found she had the best milk and the sweetest that ever I had drunk. Sire, I lived thus while my food lasted, and my son was so well fed that he shows it still, I thank God. But when my food was gone I grew weak, and one day as I was looking out of the hole in our tree I saw a great stag going by, and I was so hungry, after living a long while on milk, that I cried out: 'Oh Lord God, how I wish that I had a steak from that stag, well cooked!' The unicorn overheard me; she dashed out of the hollow tree, made after the stag, and cut him in two with a single blow of her horn.'

To make this delightful but rambling story as short as possible, the unicorn helped the dwarf gather firewood for cooking the stag, she helped him build a hut of boughs, she slew for him many other beasts as the needs of his larder required them. The child thrived mightily on unicorn milk, and when he was weaned the dwarf fed him on the flesh of bears. Before long he had grown into a giant, able to uproot huge trees at a single jerk, and finally he built the square red tower, making it very tall and without doors or windows so that wild beasts would not eat the father while the giant boy was off at play. And everywhere he went the mother unicorn went with him. While Arthur stands at the foot of the tower talking up to the dwarf, this son arrives, carrying a freshly killed bear in one hand and his club in the other. Introductions are made, the giant lifts Arthur to the top of the tower, and the three dine off the bear, the giant standing on the ground alongside. Next morning the giant and the unicorn drag Arthur's ship off the sands and the whole company sets sail for Windsor Castle. *Cy finit le conte du papegaulx.'"* (p. 59-60.)

"Returning to the Near East, one finds a similar abundance of unicorns, either seen or surmised. One John of Hesse, a priest who visited the Holy Land in 1389, had the good fortune not only to see one but to witness the water-conning performance in actual operation. Felix Fabri, who made pilgrimage to the Holy Land a century later saw, on September 20, 1483, with his own eyes- as did all the members of his company- a unicorn standing on a hill near Mount Sinai, and he observed it carefully for a long time. Lewis Vartoman, regarded for centuries as an exceptionally veracious traveler, gives a careful description of two unicorns that he says he saw at Mecca about the middle of the sixteenth century- but it is to be observed that these two had been sent to the Sultan as a present by the King of Abyssinia. Vincent Le Blanc, who set out on his travels in 1567- at the age of fourteen- saw only one unicorn at Mecca, the other one mentioned by Vartoman having died, but by way of atonement he saw two at the Court of Pegu.

Not to make too intolerably long a list, there is the unicorn of Tartary reported by a British traveler of the eighteenth century and explained one hundred and fifty years later by Lieutenant-Colonel Prejevalsky. There is the unicorn of Persia, said to have been kept as a pet by the Sophy in his private gardens at Samarkand. There is the unicorn of the Carpathians made known by Antony Scheneberger in a letter quoted by Conrad Gesner. There is the unicorn of India, distinct from the rhinoceros, clearly depicted on a map of the Orient published with the English translation of Linschoeten's Voyages. There is the unicorn of Poland reported by Aldrovandus, the unicorn of Scandinavia of which we learn in the *Historia Naturalis* of Johnston, the unicorn of Florida made known to Europe by the Spanish conquistadors, the unicorn of the

FOLK MAGIC, SUPERSTITION, AND CHARMS

Canadian border described by Olfert Dapper, and finally there is the unicorn of China. Chinese writers do not assert that the unicorn or ki-lin is a native of their land; on the contrary, they say that it comes from afar, presumably from heaven, and only at long intervals of time. They regard it, so to speak, as an intermittent animal, and its appearance on earth is considered a certain omen of a beneficent reign or of the birth of some great man comparable with a good emperor in importance. According to the testimony of Tse-Tche-t'ongkien-kang-mou, the ki-lin was first seen in the year 2697 B.C., in the palace of the Emperor Hoang-ti, on which occasion it was a truthful prophet of national felicity. Another appeared to the mother of Confucius just before the sage's birth, holding in its mouth a great tablet of jade on which there was engraved a *dithyramb* in praise of the man her son was to become. Events of this sort have occurred so many times and the prophecy has always been so unerring that pictures of the unicorn are now pinned or pasted in the womens quarters of millions of Chinese houses in the hope that they may exert prenatal influence and induce the birth of great men, or at least of boys rather than of girls. They are also affixed to the red chair in which the bride is borne to her husband's house, and the gods that oversee the distribution of desirable babies are often depicted riding upon the ki-lin. To say of any man that a ki-lin appeared at the time of his birth is the highest form of flattery.

The question is asked in the Li-Ki: 'What were the four intelligent creatures?' and the answer is given: 'They were the Phoenix, the Tortoise, the Dragon, and the Ki-lin.' The last, though not so popular as the dragon, is commonly regarded as the king of beasts. No hunter has ever killed one; and it is seldom captured or even wounded, although we are told that one was injured by a hunter just before the death of Confucius. Like an exceptionally good Buddhist, the ki-lin eats no living thing, either animal or vegetable, so that its diet is severely restricted. It will not even tread upon an insect or a living blade of grass. It has the body of a stag, the hoof of a horse-

conforming in these respects to the European tradition- the tail of an ox, and a single horn twelve feet long springing from the middle of its brow, which has at the end a fleshy growth. The most significant thing about the ki-lin's physical appearance, however, is the fact that he is resplendent in the five sacred colors, which are the symbols of his perfection.

The ki-lin is supposed to spring from the center of the earth, and perhaps he was originally a representative of the earthy element as the phoenix represents fire, the dragon air, and the tortoise water. All commentators enlarge upon the excellence of his character. He knows good from evil, is reverential towards his parents and piously attached to the memory of all his ancestors; he is harmless, beneficent, and gentle, the fleshy tip of his horn indicating clearly that that otherwise formidable member has only symbolic and aesthetic uses. Like the Western unicorn, he keeps the dignity and the mystery of solitude, never mingling promiscuously even with those of his own kind and never treading upon soil tainted by the human foot unless he comes on a mission. He is not violently haled by hunters into the court of the sovereign, but arrives as one king visiting another. Unlike the Western unicorn, the ki-lin has never had commercial value; no drug is made of any part of his body; he exists for his own sake and not for the medication, enrichment, entertainment, or even edification of mankind. We must infer that this Oriental unicorn was conceived on a higher plane of civilization than that which produced the European legend. Our Western unicorn does us credit in many ways, but when we compare him with the ki-lin we see that there is after all a good deal of violence and deceit and calculation implicit in the stories we have told of him. The ki-lin legend was developed by men who had got beyond fear and calculation in their attitude toward wild nature- by men not unlike those who painted the pictures and wrote the poetry of the Sung period in which Nature is loved for her own sufficient self almost a thousand years before the West learned to look at her without terror." (p. 66-68.)

NATURE WORSHIP
Hargrave(?) 1891

"At Mendes, female goats were also held sacred, as symbols of the passive generative attribute; and on Grecian monuments of art, we often find capine satyrs of that sex. The fable of Jupiter having been suckled by a goat, probably arose from some emblematic composition, the true explanation of which was only known to the initiated. Such was Juno Sospita of Lanuvium, near Rome, whose goat-skin dress signified the same as her title; and who, on a votive car of very ancient Etruscan work found near Perugia, appears exactly in the form described by Cicero, as the associate of Hercules dressed in the lion's skin, or the Destroyer." (p. 24.)

"The reverence paid to fish of different kinds by the Egyptians and some other ancient nations was very marked. Historians say that all the natives of the river were in some degree esteemed sacred. In many parts the people did not feed upon them. The priests in particular never tasted fish ; and this on account of their imputed sanctity, for they were sometimes looked upon as sacred emblems; at other times worshiped as real deities. One species of fish was styled Oxurunchus; and there was a city of the name, built in honor of it, and a temple where this fish was publicly worshiped. Nor was the veneration confined to this place, but prevailed in many other parts of Egypt. A fish called Phagrus was worshiped at Syene; as the Mseotis was at Elephantis. The Lepidotus had the like reverence paid to it; as had also the Eel; being each sacred to the god Nilus.

This is ridiculed in a passage, which has been often quoted, from the ancient comedian Antiphanes; who mentions, that an eel by the Egyptians was reverenced equally with the gods. Another comedian says that they esteemed it as one of their supreme deities; and he at the same time exposes their folly with some humor. A Grecian is made to address himself to an Egyptian; and he accordingly says; 'It is impossible for me to ride in the same troop with you; for our notions and manners are diametrically opposite. You pay adoration to an ox; I kill and sacrifice it to the gods. You esteem an eel to be a very great divinity. I only think it the best dish that comes upon the table. You worship a dog. I whip him handsomely; especially if I find the cur purloining my dinner.' Here it is proper to take notice, that there was a female deity called Athor in Egypt; but in Syria Atar-Cetus, or Atargatis; and abbreviated, Dercetus and Derceti. This personage was supposed to have been of old preserved by means of a fish; and was represented one half under that form; and the other half as a woman. She was esteemed to be the same as the Aphrodite of the Greeks and the Venus of the Romans, whose origin was from the sea. In consequence of this, wherever her worship prevailed, fish were esteemed sacred ; and the inhabitants would not feed upon them. This was the case at Edessa, called Hierapolis, where Atargatis or Derceto was held in particular veneration. Xenophon in his march through these parts observed, in a river called Chains, many large fishes, which appeared tame, and were never taken for food; the natives esteeming them as gods.

Lucian tells us, that this worship was of great antiquity; and was introduced into these parts from Egypt. The same custom seems to have been kept up in Babylonia; but what was of more consequence to the Israelites, it prevailed within their own borders. Dagon of Asdod, or Azotus, was the same deity; and represented under a like figure as Atargatis. The same rites and abstinence were observed also at Ascalon. Diodorus Siculus speaks of this city, which he places in Syria, rather than Palestine; at no great distance from which he says was a large lake, abounding with fishes. Near it was a noble temple of the goddess Derceto, whom they represented with the face of a woman, but from thence downwards, under the figure of a fish. The history of Derceto in this place was, that she threw herself into this lake, and was changed to a fish. On which account the inhabitants of Ascalon, and of some parts of Syria, abstained from fish; and held those of the lake as so many deities. However strange this idolatry may appear, yet we see how very far it reached; and with what a reverence it was attended. It was to be found not only in Syria, which was sufficiently near, but in the borders of Lebanon; also at Ascalon, Ashdod, and Joppa; which cities were within the precincts of the tribes of Dan and Judah." (p. 26-28.)

OPHIOLATREIA
Hargrave(?) 1889

"Some persons are disposed to attribute to the Serpent, as a religious emblem, an origin decidedly phallic. Mr C. S. Wake takes a contrary view, and says: 'So far as I can make out the serpent symbol has not a direct Phallic reference, nor is its attribute of wisdom the most essential. The idea most intimately associated with this animal was that of life, not present merely, but continued, and probably everlasting. Thus the snake Bai was figured as Guardian of the doorways of the Egyptian Tombs which represented the mansions of heaven. A sacred serpent would seem to have been kept in all the Egyptian temples, and we are told that many of the subjects, in the tombs of the kings at Thebes in particular, show the importance it was thought to enjoy in a future state. Crowns, formed of the Asp or sacred Thermuthis, were given to sovereigns and divinities, particularly to Isis, and these no doubt were intended to symbolize eternal life. Isis was a goddess of life and healing and the serpent evidently belonged to her in that character, seeing that it was the symbol also of other deities with the like attributes.

Thus, on papyri it encircles the figure of Harpocrates, who was identified with Aesculapius; while not only was a great serpent kept alive in the great temple of Serapis, but on later monuments this god is represented by a great serpent with or without a human head. Mr. Fergusson, in accordance with his peculiar theory as to the origin of serpent worship, thinks this superstition characterized the old Turanaian (or rather let us say Akkadian) empire of Chaldea, while tree-worship was more a characteristic of the later Assyrian Empire. This opinion is no doubt correct, and it means really that the older race had that form of faith with which the serpent was always indirectly connected- adoration of the male principle of generation, the principal phase of which was probably ancestor worship, while the latter race adored the female principle, symbolized by the sacred tree, the Assyrian 'grove.' The 'tree of life,' however, undoubtedly had reference to the male element, and we may well imagine that originally the fruit alone was treated as symbolical of the opposite element.'

Mr. J. H. Rivett-Carnac, in his paper printed in the journal of the Asiatic Society of Bengal, entitled 'The Snake Symbol in India,' suggests that the serpent is a symbol of the phallus. He says: 'The serpent appears on the prehistoric cromlechs and menhirs of Europe, on which I believe the remains of phallic worship may be traced. What little attention I have been able to give to the serpent symbol has been chiefly in its connection with the worship of Mahadeo or Siva, with a view to ascertain whether the worship of the snake and that of Mahadeo or the phallus may be considered identical, and whether the presence of the serpent on the prehistoric remains of Europe can be shown to support my theory, that the markings on the cromlechs and menhirs are indeed the traces of this form of worship, carried to Europe from the East by the tribes whose remains are buried beneath the tumuli.

During my visits to Benares, the chief center of Siva worship in India, I have always carefully searched for the snake symbol. On the most ordinary class of 'Mahadeo,' a rough stone placed on end supposed to represent the phallus, the serpent is not generally seen. But in the temples and in the better class of shrines which abound in the city and neighborhood the snake is generally found encircling the phallus. The tail of the snake is sometimes carried down the Yoni, and in one case I found two snakes on a shrine thus depicted. In the Benares bazaar I once came across a splendid metal cobra, the head erect and hood expanded, so made as to be placed around or above a stone or metal 'Mahadeo.' It is now in England. The attitude of the cobra when excited and the expansion of the head will suggest the reason for this snake representing Mahadeo and the phallus.'" (p. 16-18.)

"There was another similar character in Yucatan, called Ku, Kulcan or Cuculcan, another in Nicaragua named Theotbilake, son of their principal god Thomathoyo, and another in Colombia bearing the name of Bochia. Peru and Guatemala furnish similar traditions, as do also Brazil, the nations of the Tamanac race, Florida, and various savage tribes of the West. The serpent, as we show elsewhere, was an emblem both of Quetzalcoatl and of Ku Kulcan- a fact which gives some importance to the statement of Cabrera that Votan of Guatemala as above was represented to be a serpent, or of serpent origin. Torquemada states, that the images of Huitzlipochtli of Mexico, Quetzalcoatl, and Tlaloc were each represented with a golden serpent, bearing different symbolical sacrificial allusions. He also assures us that serpents often entered into the symbolical sacrificial ceremonies of the Mexicans, and presents the following example:

'Among the many sacrifices which these Indians made, there was one which they performed in honor of the mountains, by forming serpents out of wood or of the roots of the trees, to which they affixed serpents' heads, and also dolls of the same, which they called Ecatotowin, which figures of serpents and fictitious children they covered with dough, named by them Tzoalli, composed of the seeds of Bledos, and placed them on supports of wood, carved in the representation of hills or mountains, on the tops of which they fixed them. This was the kind of offering which they made to the mountains and high bills.'

The mother of Huitzlipochtli was a priestess of Tezcatlipoca (a cleanser of the temple, says Ganla) named Coatlantona, Coatlcue, or Coatlcyue (serpent of the temple or serpent woman). She was extremely devoted to the gods, and one day when walking in the temple, she beheld, descending in the air, a ball made of variously colored feathers. She placed it in her girdle, became at once pregnant, and afterwards was delivered of Mexitli or Huitzlipochtli, full armed, with a spear in one hand, a shield in the other, and a crest of green feathers on his head. He became, according to some, their leader into Anahuac, guiding them to the place where Mexico is built. His statue was of gigantic size, and covered with ornaments each one of which had its significance.

He was depicted placed upon a seat, from the four corners of which issued four large serpents. 'His body,' says Gomeza, 'was beset with pearls, precious stones and gold, and for collars and chains around his neck ten hearts of men made of gold. It had also a counterfeit visage, with eyes of glass, and in its neck death painted, all of which things had their considerations and meanings.' It was to him in his divine character of the destroyer that the bloodiest sacrifices of Mexico were performed. His wife, Teoyaonliqui (from Teo, sacred or divine; Yaoyotl, war; and Miqui, to kill) was represented as a figure bearing the full breasts of a woman, literally enveloped in serpents, and ornamented with feathers, shells, and the teeth and claws of a tiger. She had a necklace composed of six hands. Around her waist is a belt to which death's heads are attached. One of her statues, a horrible figure, still exists in the city of Mexico. It is carved from a solid block of basalt, and is nine feet in height and five and a half in breadth. It is not improbable that the serpent-mother of Huitzlipochtli was an impersonation of the great female serpent Cinacohuatl, the wife of Tonacatlecoatl, the serpent-father of Quetzalcoatl." (p. 62-63.)

"Here we may suitably introduce the tradition of a great serpent, which is to this day, current among a large portion of the Indians of the Algonquin stock. It affords some curious parallelisms with the allegorical relations of the old world. The Great Teacher of the Algonquins, Manabozho, is always placed in antagonism to a great serpent, a spirit of evil, who corresponds very nearly with the Egyptian Typhon, the Indian Kaliya, and the Scandinavian Midgard. He is also connected with the Algonquin notions of a deluge; and as Typhon is placed in opposition to Osiris or Apollo, Kaliya to Surya or the Sun, and Midgard to Wodin or Odin, so does he bear a corresponding relation to Manabozho. The conflicts between the two are frequent; and although the struggles are sometimes long and doubtful, Manabozho is usually successful against his adversary. One of these contests involved the destruction of the earth by water, and its reproduction by the powerful and beneficent Manabozho.

The tradition in which this grand event is embodied was thus related by Kah-gega-gah-boowh, a chief of the Ojibwa. In all of its the Indians, and scattered all over the Algonquin territories. One day returning to his lodge, from a long journey, Manabozho missed from it his young cousin, who resided with him, he called his name aloud, but received no answer. He looked around on the sand for the tracks of his feet, and he there, for the first time, discovered the trail of Meshekenabek, the serpent. He then knew that his cousin had been seized by his great enemy. He armed himself, and followed on his track, he passed the great river, and crossed mountains and valleys to the shores of the deep and gloomy lake now called Manitou Lake, Spirit Lake, or the Lake of Devils. The trail of Meshekennbek led to the edge of the water. At the bottom of this lake was the dwelling of the serpent, and it was filled with evil spirits- his attendants and companions. Their forms were monstrous and terrible, but most, like their master, bore the semblance of serpents. In the center of this horrible assemblage was Meshekenabek himself, coiling his volumes around the hapless cousin of Manabozho. His head was red as with blood, and his eyes were fierce and glowed like fire. His body was all over armed with hard and glistening scales of every shade and color.

Manabozho looked down upon the writhing spirits of evil, and he vowed deep revenge. He directed the clouds to disappear from the heavens, the winds to be still, and the air to become stagnant over the lake of the manitous, and bade the sun shine upon it with all its fierceness; for thus he sought to drive his enemy forth to seek the cool shadows of the trees, that grew upon its banks, so that he might be able to take vengeance upon him. Meanwhile, Manabozho, seized his bow and arrows and placed himself near the spot where he deemed the serpents would come to enjoy the shade. He then transferred himself into the broken stump of a withered tree, so that his enemies might not discover his presence. The winds became still, and the sun shone hot on the lake of the evil manitous. By and by the waters became troubled, and bubbles rose to the surface, for the rays of the sun penetrated to the horrible brood within its depths. The commotion increased, and a serpent lifted its head high above the center of the lake and gazed around the shores. Directly another came to the surface, and they listened for the footsteps of Manabozho but they heard him nowhere on the face of the earth, and they said one to the other, 'Manabozho sleeps.' And then they plunged again beneath the waters, which seemed to hiss as they closed over them.

It was not long before the lake of manitous became more troubled than before, it boiled from its very depths, and the hot waves dashed wildly against the rocks on its shores. The commotion increased, and soon Meshekenabek, the Great Serpent, emerged slowly to the surface, and moved towards the shore. His blood-red crest glowed with a deeper hue, and the reflection from his glancing scales was like the blinding glitter of a sleet covered forest beneath the morning sun of winter. He was followed by the evil spirits, so great a number that they covered the shores of the lake with their foul trailing carcasses. They saw the broken, blasted stump into which Manabozho had transformed himself, and suspecting it might he one of his disguises, for they knew his cunning, one of them approached, and wound his tail around it, and sought to drag it down. But Manabozho stood firm, though he could hardly refrain from crying aloud, for the tail of the monster tickled his sides. The Great Serpent wound his vast folds among the trees of the forest, and the rest also sought the shade, while one was left to listen for the steps of Manabozho.

When they all slept, Manabozho silently drew an arrow from his quiver, he placed it in his bow, and aimed it where he saw the heart beat against the sides of the Great Serpent. He launched it, and with a howl that shook the mountains and startled the wild beasts in their caves, the monster awoke, and, followed by its frightful companions, uttering mingled sounds of rage and terror, plunged again into the lake. Here they vented their fury on the helpless cousin of Manabozho, whose body they tore into a thousand fragments, his mangled lungs rose to the surface, and covered it with whiteness. And this is the origin of the foam on the water. When the Great Serpent knew that he was mortally wounded, both he and the evil spirits around him were rendered tenfold more terrible by their great wrath and they rose to overwhelm Manabozho. The water of the lake swelled upwards from its dark depths, and with a sound like many thunders, it rolled madly on its track, bearing the rocks and trees before it with resistless fury. High on the crest of the foremost wave, black as the midnight, rode the writhing form of the wounded Meshekenabek, and red eyes glazed around him, and the hot breaths of the monstrous brood hissed fiercely above the retreating Manabozho. Then thought Manabozho of his Indian children, and he ran by their villages, and in a voice of alarm bade them flee to the mountains, for the Great Serpent was deluging the earth in his expiring wrath, sparing no living thing. The Indians caught up their children, and wildly sought safety where he bade them. But Manabozho continued his flight along the base of the western hills, and finally took refuge on a high mountain beyond Lake Superior, far towards the north. There he found many men and animals who had fled from the flood that already covered the valleys and plains, and even the highest hills. Still the waters continued to rise, and soon all the mountains were overwhelmed save that on which stood Manabozho. Then he gathered together timber, and made a raft, upon which the men and women, and the animals that were with him, all placed themselves. No sooner had they done so, than the rising floods closed over the mountain and they floated alone on the surface of the waters; and thus they floated for many days, and some died, and the rest became sorrowful, and reproached Manabozho that he did not disperse the waters and renew the earth that they might live. But though he knew that his great enemy was by this time dead, yet could not Manabozho renew the world unless he had some earth in his hands wherewith to begin the work. And this he explained to those that were with him, and he said that were it ever so little, even a few grains of earth, then could he disperse the waters and renew the world. Then the beaver volunteered to go to the bottom of the deep, and get some earth, and they all applauded her design. She plunged in, they waited long, and when she returned she was dead; they opened her hands but there was no earth in them. 'Then,' said the otter, 'will I seek the earth:' and the bold swimmer dived from the raft. The otter was gone still longer than the beaver, but when he returned to the surface he too was dead, and there was no earth in his claws. 'Who shall find the earth?' exclaimed all those left on the raft, 'now that the beaver and the otter are dead?' and they desponded more than before, repeating, 'Who shall find the earth?' 'That will I,' said the muskrat, and he quickly disappeared between the logs of the raft. The muskrat was gone very long much longer than the otter, and it was thought he would never return, when he suddenly rose near by, but he was too weak to speak, and he swam slowly towards the raft. He had hardly got upon it when he too died from his great exertion. They opened his little hands and there, clasped closely between the fingers, they found a few grains of fresh earth. These Manabozho carefully collected and dried them in the sun, and then he rubbed them into a fine powder in his palms, and, rising up, he blew them abroad upon the waters. No sooner was this done than the flood began to subside, and soon the trees on the mountains and hills emerged from the deep, and the plains and the valleys came in view and the waters disappeared from the land leaving no trace but a thick sediment, which was the dust that Manabozho had blown abroad from the raft.

Then it was found that Meshekenabek, the Great Serpent, was dead, and that the evil manitous, his companions, had returned to the depths of the lake of spirits, from which, for the fear of Manabozho, they never more dared to come forth. And in gratitude to the beaver, the otter, and the muskrat, those animals were ever after held sacred by the Indians, and they became their brethren, and they never killed nor molested them until the medicine of the stranger made them forget their relations and turned their hearts to ingratitude." (p. 90-95.)

THE PETIT ALBERT
18th Century

"To Ward Off Wolves

If you wear on your body the eyes and heart of a dog that died by violence, you will not need to fear wolves, and they will flee like cowardly rabbits. If you hang the tail of a wolf that was killed in a fight in the manger or a barn or with your sheep, wolves will stay away from them. The same effect happens in a village if you bury some wolf bones under the streets. I read in the writings of one naturalist, a very surprising way to take in large numbers of wolves, even to depopulate an entire country swarming with them; you must obtain a good amount of fish, called *biemmi* or marine wolf, which are carnivorous, and after having cleaned well the meat and removed the scales, they should be crushed in a mortar with lamb flesh, and then, you must bring this mixture into the woods where the wolves reside. Create a large coal fire to the opposition of the wind; that is to say, the wind must blow into the wolf-infested area, so that the smoke will billow towards the wolves. They will be attracted to the burning bait, consume the fish, and fall into a coma, often dying.

There are so many books that are filled with secrets to destroy pests, and I do not think that it is necessary to list many here in this book, but these kinds of secrets that have become too common to ignore them. So I will move on to the most curious things that will satisfy the reader." (p. 31-32.)

POW WOWS
John George Hohman, 1822

"*To make chickens lay many eggs*

Take the dung of rabbits, pound it to powder, mix it with bran, wet the mixture till it forms lumps, and feed your chickens with it, and they will keep on laying a great many eggs." (p. 31.)

"*A good method of destroying rats and mice*

Every time you bring grain into your barn, you must, in putting down the three first sheaves, repeat the following words: 'Rats and mice, these three sheaves I give to you, in order that you may not destroy any of my wheat.' The name of the kind of grain must also be mentioned." (p. 35)

SIGNS, OMENS, AND SUPERSTITIONS
Astra Cielo, 1918

"*Animal Portents*

The following are believed to foretell death: Rats leaving a house; a hare or white rabbit crossing your path; a cow lowing three times in your face; a shrew mouse running over your foot.

FOLK MAGIC, SUPERSTITION, AND CHARMS

It is unlucky to keep a kitten born in May. It should be drowned, as a May cat is supposed to suck a child's breath.

Goslings hatched in May bring no luck to the owner.

It is unlucky to bid a price for an animal that is not for sale. The animal is apt to die within a month.

To covet another's beast will bring you bad luck. If a pig is killed while the moon is waning, it will be unprofitable and the bacon will shrink in the pot.

A gray horse brings good luck. Spit on the little finger and rub it on the horse, and money will come to you.

If you see a young spring lamb with the head towards you, it means good fortune. It foretells bad luck if rats gnaw one's clothing.

It is unlucky to kill a cricket. These insects were esteemed by the ancients as a symbol of hospitality. Their singing was often used to foretell good or bad events.

A hare crossing the path of a traveler is a sign of bad fortune. A white hare, however, is regarded as a good sign.

A pig appearing to a traveler is a good sign. If a sow be accompanied by a litter of pigs, it denotes a successful trip.

The tail of a lizard is considered a lucky mascot in France, just as is the hind leg of a rabbit in this country.

To meet a white horse is considered unlucky unless the person spits at it to avert trouble. To meet a white horse indicates that you will soon see a red-haired girl.

Rooks are believed to foretell death by leaving the

house near which they have built their nests.

Killing a spider is considered unlucky. Small spiders, called 'money-spinners,' indicate good luck, and their webs are not to be destroyed.

If black ants appear in a house it is a sign of good luck, but red ants bring misfortune.

To meet a goat unexpectedly is bad luck; to meet a sheep is a good sign." (p. 91-92.)

"*Good Omens*

'The signs are lucky all, and right.
There hath not been a voice, or flight,
Of ill presage.'
-Ben Jonson.

Happily every creature is not placed on the black list of those whose melancholy mission is to foretell calamities. There are, on the other hand, many whose purpose is said to be exactly the reverse- to augur good luck, peace, happiness; and curiously enough most of these prognosticators are birds.

The Stork, that 'emblem of true piety,' is a bird whose presence is regarded as an augury of good fortune in almost all countries where it is known. In Holland and Germany at the present day the inhabitants give the birds every encouragement to make their nests on the roofs of the houses, and fortunate is the man supposed to be whose house the storks choose for this purpose. Longfellow, in an American song, 'To the Stork,' very beautifully illustrates this belief:

'Welcome, O Stork! that dost wing
Thy flight from far away!
Thou hast brought us the signs of spring,

Thou hast made our sad hearts gay.
Descend, O Stork! descend
Upon our roof to rest;
In our ash-tree, O my friend.
My darling, make thy nest.'

In the *Golden Legend* the same poet represents the bird as a direct gift from God. Speaking of the good Prince Henry, Bertha asks:

'Did he give us the beautiful stork above
On the chimney-top, with its large round nest?'

And Gottlieb replies:

'No, not the stork. By God in heaven,
As a blessing, the dear white stork was given.'

The reverence for the stork dates back to very ancient times. The Egyptians paid it the Same reverence as the sacred Ibis; the Thessalonians were restricted from doing the bird an injury; the Romans regarded it as a bird of good augury. A Greek law compelling children to maintain their aged parents took its name from the bird, and all the numerous legends which have been woven round its name testify to its devotion, faithfulness, love, and, generally speaking, its sterling character. Was it not into a stork that the pitying gods transformed Antigone when, boastful of her beautiful hair, the jealous Juno turned her locks into writhing serpents?

As an example of the stork's devotion to its young ones, we are told that on a fire occurring in the city of Delft, the parent, after making strenuous efforts to rescue them without success, permitted herself to perish with them in the flames. The stork's faithfulness to its mate is brought out in a story that the male bird, rather than desert his partner when she was wounded at the time of migrating, spent the winter months by her side tenderly providing for her needs. Its filial devotion is said to be so great that when the parent is too old to fly the young bird carries her on his back, and supplies her with food:

> 'When age had seized and made his dam
> Unfit for flight, the grateful young one takes
> His mother on his back, provides her food,
> Repaying thus her tender care of him
> Ere he was fit to fly.'

But here, I am afraid, we are straying into the realms of fiction. While there is hardly room to doubt that the devoted bird at Delft yielded up its life in preference to deserting its young- an act of maternal solicitude which would be equaled by many a little bird in the hedgerows,- or that it watched faithfully by the side of its wounded mate, we must look with suspicion on a stork carrying its infirm old parent about like a Kaffir with a child on her hips.

Such stories as these have, no doubt, served to strengthen the Eastern belief in the stork as a bird of good augury; but there are passages in the Armenian song referred to above which seem to show that, like the swallow, the bird is welcomed more particularly as a harbinger of spring. 'Thou hast brought us the signs of spring' is very suggestive of this idea, as are also two verses descriptive of the change of weather which followed the stork's return to a warmer climate:

> 'When thou away didst go,
> Away from this tree of ours,
> The withering winds did blow.
> And dried up all the flowers.
> Dark grew the brilliant sky.
> Cloudy and dark and drear;
> They were breaking the snow on high.
> And winter was drawing near.'

'Swift-winged and pleasing harbinger of spring,' a title given by a Yorkshire poet to the Swallow, gives us a clue to the peculiar veneration in which these birds are universally held. By the ancients they were placed among those requiring special honor, the Romans believing that the spirits of departed children took up their abode in the bodies of these graceful birds, and in this way came periodically to visit their old homes. But this pretty myth only helps to strengthen the supposition that it is as 'a harbinger of spring' that the swallow obtains its title of a bird of good augury, and this belief is implanted deep in the hearts of even little children. Dryden tells us that 'Swallows are unlucky birds to kill,' and Pope that 'Children sacred held a Martin's nest;' and any schoolboy, though perhaps he may not be able to give a reason for his belief, will tell us that to destroy a swallow's nest will bring 'bad luck.'

Among young people the ancient fable which tells us why;

'Progne makes on chimney-tops her moan.
And hovers o'er the palace once her own,'

...can have no influence over their feelings; nor in England is the swallow, as it is in Sweden, associated in any way with the Crucifixion of our Lord. In addition to believing that bad luck will result from killing a swallow or destroying its nest, many people believe that precisely the reverse will obtain if swallows build under their eaves, and very great care is taken to prevent the birds from being frightened or molested. There is a passage in Hood which seems to refer to this belief:

'But bid the sacred swallow haunt his eaves
To guard his roof from lightning and from thieves.'

While touring in Turkey some years ago, I was very much interested in a pair of swallows which had the temerity to build a nest on a bracket inside a coffee-house near

Constantinople. The bracket, which was not more than seven feet from the ground, had apparently been placed on the wall for the birds' special benefit, and they showed their appreciation by treating the host and his customers as confidential promoters of the scheme. The swallows left and entered the apartment by means of the doorway, which was also used by the customers,' and so little did they fear 'the unspeakable Turk,' that they frequently passed close to his face when they happened to meet him coming in or going out. The presence of the birds seemed to give the proprietor immense satisfaction, and I have no doubt he would stoutly have prevented their receiving any molestation; but whether he considered them harbingers of 'good luck' I cannot say.

Yet while it is not every one who desires to have swallows nesting on their buildings, chiefly in consequence of the dirt which is made by the birds and their young, there are very few people who would wantonly break their nests or frighten them away. 'When they go they take your luck away with them,' is a common saying. Not more than a few months ago I was told about a farmer who had destroyed a number of swallows' nests on his house and barns, ever since which time the swallows had refused to colonize on his farm buildings, and he had experienced a series of misfortunes. Whether the original builders of a nest which has been destroyed will return at another season to the place of the depredation seems to be somewhat a moot question. I have known of nests remaining in a broken state for many summers after they have been destroyed, the swallows apparently refusing, through fear or vexation, to rebuild the old habitations. That sometimes swallows will repair old nests which have ruthlessly been damaged has been amply proved, but it is very doubtful whether the birds have been the same as those which built them in the first instance. While;

'The martin and the swallow
Are God Almighty's bow and arrow,'

It is also said that:

'The robin and the wren
Are God Almighty's cock and hen;'

And nothing but ill fortune would attend the callous man who dared to do an injury to our pugnacious little friend the Redbreast, and his tiny wife Jenny Wren.

'Him that harries their nest,
Never shall his soul have rest,'

...Says a popular rhyme. Another tells us that:

'If you go to catch a robin.
You will come back a-sobbing.'

Or in similar words:

'The red on the breast of a robin that's sought,
Brings blood to the snarer by whom it is caught;'

...or still further:

'A robin in a cage
Sets all heaven in a rage.'

Truly, a 'robin in a cage' is a rare as well as an unnatural and disagreeable sight. I shall not soon forget the displeasing impression made upon my own feelings, and upon those of many others, on seeing a robin imprisoned in a pretty painted cage in a side-show. The bird seemed altogether out of place- a little martyr, a fluffy, pathetic appeal to our tenderest natures. Yet, why so more than any other bird 'fastened and imprisoned behind bars.' Can it be that the melancholy fate of the 'breast burned bird' told in the tales of our childhood still linger with us and bring forth our compassion? If so, long may they linger and create sympathies and tender feelings which in these days are all too rare. Happily the pretty redbreast, stained with the blood of our Redeemer (so fables tell us), is yet to be seen in our crofts and on our window-sills, and the appearance of the pugnacious little visitor in our rooms is accepted both as a sign of confidence in our goodwill and an augury of good fortune.

The Cuckoo- 'Darling of the spring,' as Wordsworth endearingly calls it, is another bird whose name is synonymous with good luck, and this very probably because, like the swallow and the stork, its appearance is significant of spring's sweet advent.

> 'Hark, how the jolly cuckoos sing
> 'Cuckoo!' to welcome in the spring.'
> -John Lyly.

Whatever you may wish, folks say, when first you hear the cuckoo's call, your wish will be gratified. But a very ancient tradition insists that in order to obtain good luck, especially in affairs of love, it is necessary to hear the notes of the nightingale first. To go back only to the days of Chaucer, we learn:

> 'How lovers had a tokening,
> And among hem it was a commune tale
> That it were good to here the nightingale
> Rather than the leud cuckow sing.'

And the poet tells how, half-asleep and half-awake:

> 'I hearde sing
> The sorry bird, the leud cuckow.
> And that was on a tree right fast by,
> But who was than evill apaid but I?
> 'Now God,' quod I, 'that died on the crois,
> Yeve sorrow on thee, and on thy leud vois.
> Full little joy have I now of thy cry.'

And as I with the cuckow thus gan chide,
I heard in the next bush beside
A nightingale so lustely sing
That with her clere voice she made ring
Through all the greene wood wide.

'Ah, good nightingale,' quod I then,
'A little hast thou ben too long hen.
For here hath ben the leud cuckow,
And songen songs rather than hast thou,
I pray to God evill fire her bren."

Milton, in his 'Ode to the Nightingale,' referring to the same superstition, writes:

'O nightingale, that on yonder blooming spray
Warblest at eve, when all the woods are still:
Thou with fresh hopes the lover's heart dost fill,
While the jolly Hours lead on propitious May.
The liquid notes that close the eyes of day.
First heard before the shallow cuckoo's bill,
Portend success in love; O if Jove's will
Have linked that amorous power to thy soft lay,
Now timely sing, ere the rude bird of hate
Foretell my hopeless doom in some grove nigh.'

Chaucer's reference to the cuckoo as a 'leud bird,' and Milton's condemnation of it as 'a rude bird of hate' arise, no doubt, from its association with unfaithfulness in marriage. Probably its own singular habit of leaving its eggs to be hatched by other birds has been the origin of this association. Chaucer represents the bird as cynical in the extreme in its view of love and matrimony. When the nightingale has so beautifully been singing of the virtues which love engenders, the cuckoo sarcastically observes:

'Nightingale, thou speakest wonder faire,

But for all that is the sooth contraire.
For love is in young folke but rage,
And in old folke a great dotage,
Who most it useth, most shall enpaire.'

The cry of the cuckoo is supposed to denote mockery, and one of our old English words having this significance is derived from the Latin word cuculus- a cuckoo. Shakespeare, in the song which closes *Love's Labour's Lost,* uses the note of the cuckoo to convey this meaning:

'When daisies pied, and violets blue,
And lady-smocks all silver white,
And cuckoo-buds of yellow hue,
Do paint the meadows with delight,
The cuckoo then, on every tree,
Mocks married men; for thus sings he.
Cuckoo;
Cuckoo, cuckoo: O word of fear,
Unpleasing to a married ear!'

Poor cuckoo! What senseless havoc does man's imagination make of Natural History! Through the construction of a stupid fable the cuckoo's 'jolly voice' becomes 'leud', 'hated', and 'a word of fear.' Still, not so, I hope, to most of us. We listen with a rejoicing sense of approaching summer, with all its full verdure and warmth, as once again the curious voice of the hidden bird rings out. And among the poets, too, the bird is not wanting for friendship. Spenser called it 'The merry Cuckow, messenger of spring.' John Lyly describes it as 'jolly;' Wordsworth 'delights' in the voice of the 'blithe new-comer;' and John Logan, the Scotch poet, in a gem of poetry devoted to a eulogy of the bird, hails it as 'beauteous stranger of the grove.' The poem is so delicate and true to nature that I would like to reprint it here in its entirety; three verses, however, must suffice:

'Hail, beauteous stranger of the grove!

Thou messenger of spring!
Now Heaven repairs thy rural seat.
And woods thy welcome sing.
What time the daisy decks the green,
Thy certain voice we hear;
Hast thou a star to guide thy path,
Or mark the rolling year?
Delightful visitant! with thee
I hail the time of flowers,
And hear the sound of music sweet
From birds among the bowers.'

Similar to the expression of a wish on hearing the cuckoo call is the belief that 'any wish will come true' if made on seeing the first lamb of the season, and there is no reservation in this case about seeing or hearing any other animal first. This wholesale kind of wishing, however, is hardly to be commended, for though it may be lucky for the person expressing the wish, it may be very unlucky for other people. Then it is also said that a piebald or white horse is an animal which brings good luck; but some people add that you must express your wish before you think of its tail, a reservation which makes the act of wishing an impossibility. I can well remember how, when I was a schoolboy, it was our invariable custom to expectorate over our little fingers on seeing a white or piebald horse in order to secure good luck.

From the results up to date I must admit I have not very abundant faith in this particular form of superstition. Perhaps, however, I thought of their tails! A black Cat without a single white hair in its fur is almost universally regarded as a 'lucky animal,' and quite a large number of people keep a black cat for no other reason than to ensure prosperity. Woe be to the foolish person who turns one of these sable augurs from his door; and woe, some people say, to those from whose door the animal turns of its own accord. Quite recently a lady told me with great distress she had lost her cat. 'I should not have minded,' she said, 'but it was perfectly black.'

The following instance of superstitious belief in black cats appeared in the March (1903) issue of the 'Badminton Magazine,' the subject of the remarks being Prince Ranjitsinhji:

'The Prince has a great superstition in black cats, and the appearance of one at a shooting gathering serves to convince him in advance of a fine morning plus a fine bag, and singularly enough, it always turns out so. Twice in succession, he claims, has the timely appearance of a black cat been instrumental in winning a county match for Sussex in addition to other occasions.'

A superstitious belief in cats, black or otherwise, is of very great antiquity. Among the Egyptians the animals were regarded with the utmost reverence, and their mummified remains, a cargo of which was imported to England not many years ago, are frequently found in the same tombs as their worshipers. In witchcraft and soothsaying cats have always played no unimportant part, and wherever we see a picture or description of a witch's hovel, there too we shall certainly find portrayed her companion in darkness, a black cat.

> 'In a dirtie Haire-lace
> She leads on a brace
> Of black-bore-cats to attend her
> Who scratch at the Moone,
> And threaten at noone
> Of night from Heaven to render her.'
> -Herrick, *The Hag*.

One of the special ingredients in the filthy concoctions with which these hags were supposed to work their villainy was the brains of a black cat. Ben Jonson, in his Masque of Queens, mentions this ingredient in the song sung by the witches:

'I from the jaws of a gardener's bitch,
Did snatch these bones and then leaped the ditch:
Yet I went back to the house again,
Killed the black cat, and here's the brain.'

A well-known superstition existing at the present day is that a very minute species of Spider, commonly known as the 'Money-spider' or 'Money-spinner,' will, by creeping upon one's hand, bring good fortune- for preference a legacy. Even timid ladies, who would fall in a faint were any other creeping thing to touch them, will allow the little 'Money-spinner' to crawl upon them with impunity, hoping that by permitting it to do so some form of good luck will ensue.

While writing upon the subject of spiders it will not be out of place to mention the popular belief that to kill a spider will certainly cause rain to fall. I have met with this superstition in several parts of the country. In a small town in the West Riding of Yorkshire not long ago, I saw a youngster intently watching a spider making its way across a pavement, or 'causeway' as it is called in those parts. Presently, when the spider was about to reach a place of safety, the boy raised his foot to crush the little creature, but his nurse, who was quick enough to prevent him, cried out with some alarm, 'No, don't kill it, or we shall have rain tomorrow.'" (p. 40-52)

PLANT FOLKLORE

ANIMISM
Edward Clodd, 1905

"A recent traveler among the 'primitive pagans' of Southern Nigeria reports this speech from a native; 'Yes, we say, this is our life- the big tree. When any of us dies his spirit does not go to another country, but into the big tree; and this is why we will not have it cut. When a man is sick, or a woman wants a child, we sacrifice to the big tree, and unless Oso'wo wants the sick man, our request is granted. Oso'wo lives in the sky, and is the Big God. When any of us dies away from this place, his spirit returns to the big tree." In such customs and beliefs as these are the materials of the manifold tree-cults; of the worship and propitiation of the god in the solitary tree, the Mexican Tota, the Greek Dionysus, and the Roman Jupiter Feretrius; of the gods of sacred groves and oracles; and the materials also of the legends of the world life-tree; as the Yggdrasil of Scandinavian myth, and the giant cedar of Chaldean myth, whence perhaps that of the Hebrew Tree of Knowledge was derived." (p. 44.)

CLAVICULA SALOMONIS
17th Century

"Of Hyssop Water and its Manufacture

The water which is mentioned so often must be exorcised after this sort, upon the day of Mercury, and his hour: Take a censer with exorcised perfumes, and salt, and fill the pot full of clear water, and first hallow the salt saying:

'Sabaoth, Messias, Tetragrammaton, Emanuel, Cedron, Fortis, Janua, Turris Fortitudinis, vouchsafe to sanctify this salt.'

Which said throw it into the water, and say over it the seven psalm, and this prayer following:

'You are my God, and my rest, you are my true and right way, my help, most holy father, even as I trust in you, oh God who is the God of Abraham, the God of Isaac, and the God of Jacob; I beseech you, oh lord almighty, by the invocations and deserts of your saints: vouchsafe to bless and sanctify this water, that upon whoever it be cast, he may receive health both of body and soul. Amen.'" (p. 43.)

Note: That the name of this water relates to the literal use of hyssop, hence the mention of "exorcised perfumes." This is elaborated on:

"*Of Hyssop:*

The water being ready, make a sprinkle of verbena, valerian, fennel, sage, marjoram, and basil, and let all be put upon a hazel wand; and know that in the day of Mercury, in the morning, in the increase of the moon, it must be cut, at one cut, with the above named knife; and in that hour let the herbs be gathered; which being made, cause three masses to be said over them; which done say the gospel of Saint John, over them, afterward upon the hazel wand, wherewith you made the sprinkle, write these following characters with the needle:"

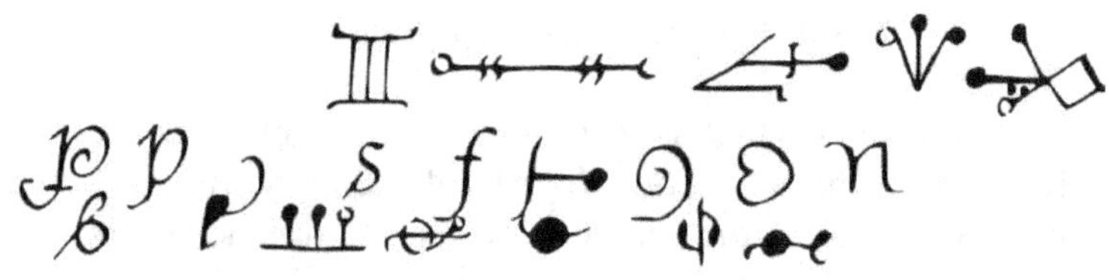

(p. 44-45.)

CULTUS ARBORUM
Hargrave(?) 1890

"The Banyan or Indian fig tree, is perhaps the most beautiful and surprising production of nature in the vegetable kingdom. Some of these trees are of an amazing size, and as they are always increasing, they may in some measure be said to be exempt from decay. Every branch proceeding from the trunk throws out its own roots, first in small fibers, at the distance of several yards from the ground. These, continually becoming thicker as they approach the earth, take root and shoot out new branches, which in time bend downwards, take root in the like manner, and produce other branches, which continue in this state of progression as long as they find soil to nourish them. The Hindus are remarkably fond of this tree, for they look upon it as an emblem of the Deity, on account of its outstretching arms and its shadowy beneficence. They almost pay divine honors, and 'find a Fane in every Grove.'

Near these trees the most celebrated pagodas are generally erected; the Brahmins spend their lives in religious solitude under their friendly shade, and the natives of all castes and tribes are fond of retreating into the cool recesses and natural bowers of this umbrageous canopy, which is impervious to the fiercest beams of the tropical sun. The particular tree here described grows on an island in the river Nerbedda, ten miles from the city of Baroach, in the province of Guzzurat, a flourishing settlement formerly in possession of the East India Company, but ceded by the government of Bengal at the treaty of peace concluded with the Mahrattas in 1783, to Mahadjee, a Mahratta chief. This tree, called in India *Cubeer Burr*, in honor of a famous saint, was much larger than it has been of late; for high floods have at different times carried away the banks of the island where it grows, and along with such parts of the tree as had extended their roots thus far; yet what has remained is about two thousand feet in circumference, measuring round the principal stems; but the hanging branches, the roots of which have not yet reached the ground, cover a much larger extent.

The chief trunks of this single tree amount to three hundred and fifty, all superior in size to the generality of our English oaks and elms; the smaller stems, forming into stronger supports, are more than three thousand; and from each of these new branches, hanging roots are proceeding, which in time will form trunks and become parents to a future progeny.' (p. 21-22.)

"'In the eighteenth century, it was remarked by Ohardin at Ispahan, that the religious Mohammedans chose rather to pray under a very old tree than in the neighboring mosque. They devoutly reverence, says he, those trees which seem to have existed during many ages, piously believing that the holy men of former times had prayed and meditated under their shade. He noticed also at Ispahan a large and ancient plane, all bristling with nails and points, and hung with rags as votive offerings from dervishes, who, like monks of the Latin church, were professed mendicants, and came under the tree to perform their devotions. He next describes another plane, said to be in his time above one thousand years old; it was black with age, and preserved with extreme care. This attention, adds he, arises from a superstitious respect entertained by the Persians for those ancient trees already mentioned. They call them *Dracte fasel* or the excellent trees, venerating them as having been miraculously preserved by God so many years, because they had afforded shade and shelter to his faithful servants, the Dervishes and others professing a religious life. Another plane, one of these excellent trees, held in veneration, to which the devout resorted, is then described by this celebrated traveler. (tome VIII., p. 187).

One, also, at Shirdz, to which they tied chaplets, amulets, and pieces of their garments; while the sick (or some friends for them) burned incense, fastened small lighted tapers to the tree, and practiced other superstitions in hopes of thereby restoring health. Throughout all Persia, adds Chardin, these *Dracte fasel* are venerated by the multitude, and they appear all stuck over with nails used in fixing in them shreds of clothes and other votive offerings. Under their shade the pious love to repose whole nights, fancying they behold resplendent lights, the souls of Aoulia or blessed saints, who had under the same trees performed their devotions. To those spirits, persons afflicted with tedious maladies devote themselves; and if they recover, the cure is attributed to their influence and proclaimed a miracle.

The plane trees of Persia, the reverence paid to them as divinities, and the worship accorded them on account of their great age, are mentioned also by others, notably by Father Angelo, who resided in the country for a considerable period. Ousley says: 'Pietro della Valle, in 1622, celebrated the great Cypress of Passa, anciently Pasagarda according to the general opinion; and, nearly two hundred years after, I beheld this beautiful tree with admiration equal to that expressed by the Italian traveler. He mentions that it was regarded with devotion by the Mohammedans; that tapers were often lighted in the capacious hollow of its trunk, as in a place worthy of veneration; the people respecting large and ancient trees, supposing them to be frequently the receptacles of blessed souls, and calling them on that account. Pir or 'aged,' a name equivalent to the Arabic Sheikh; also Imam, signifying a priest or pontiff; so they entitle those of their sect whom they imagine to have died in the odor of sanctity. Therefore when they say that such a tree or such a place is a Pir, they mean that the soul of some holy elder, a venerable personage whom they believe blessed, delights to reside in that tree or to frequent that spot. This most excellent traveler then observes that the veneration paid to trees may be considered as a remnant of ancient paganism, and aptly quotes various lines from Virgil in confirmation thereof.'" (p. 45-46.)

"The Hebrews had a sacred tree which figured in their

temple architecture along with the cherubim; it was the same sort of tree as that which had previously been in use among the Egyptians, and was subsequently, in a conventional form, adopted by the Assyrians and Persians, and eventually by the Christians, who introduced it in the mosaics of their early churches associated with their most sacred rites. This tree, which occurs also as a religious, symbol on Etruscan remains, and was abbreviated by the Greeks into a familiar ornament of their temple architecture, was the date palm, *Phoenix dactylifera.* But although the earliest known form of the Tree of Life on Egyptian monuments is the date palm, at a later period the sycamore fig tree was represented instead, and eventually even this disappeared in some instances and a female personification came in its place." (p. 73-74.)

"The oak was considered by the ancients as the emblem of hospitality; because when Jupiter and Mercury were traveling in disguise, and arrived at the cottage of Philemon, who was afterwards changed into an oak tree, they were treated with the greatest kindness. Philemon was a poor old man who lived with his wife Baucis in Phrygia, in a miserable cottage, which Jupiter, to reward his hospitality, changed into a magnificent temple, of which he made the old couple priest and priestess, granting them the only request they made to him, namely, to be permitted to die together. Accordingly, when both were grown so old as to wish for death, Jove turned Baucis into a lime tree, and Philemon into an oak; the two trees entwining their branches, and shading for more than a century the magnificent portal of the Phrygian temple." (p. 98.)

FISHES FLOWERS AND FIRE
Hargrave(?) 1890

"It would be interesting did space allow to enumerate some of the myths and legends connected with flowers, but as we have another object in view these must be allowed to pass with a mere cursory allusion. There is the Flos Adonis which perpetuates the memory of Venus's favorite, Adonis, the son of Myrrha, who was herself said to be turned into a tree called myrrh. Adonis had often been warned by Venus not to hunt wild beasts; but disregarding her advice, he was at last killed by a wild boar and was then changed by his mistress into this flower.

There was Narcissus, too, destroying himself in trying to grasp his form when reflected in the water by whose margin he was reclining. Then we have Myrtillus and the Myrtle. The father of Hippodamia declared that no one should marry his daughter who could not conquer him in a chariot race, and one of the lovers of the young lady bribed Myrtillus, who was an attendant of Aenomaus, to take out the linchpin from his master's chariot, by which means the master was killed); and Myrtillus, repenting when he saw him dead, cast himself into the sea, and was afterwards changed by Mercury into the myrtle.

A bladder campion (Silene inflata) is another curiosity. Ancient writers say that it was formerly a youth named Campion, whom Minerva employed to catch Hies for her owls to eat during the day, when their eyes did not serve them to catch food for themselves, but Campion, indulging himself with a nap when he ought to have been busy at his task, the angry goddess changed him into this flower, which still retains in its form the bladders in which Campion kept his flies, and droops its head at night when owls fly abroad and have their eyes about them.

The common clover which was much used in ancient Greek festivals, was regarded by the Germans as sacred, chiefly in its four leaved variety. There is indeed, in the vicinity of Altenburg, a superstition that if a farmer takes home with him a handful of clover taken from each of the four corners of his neighbor's field it will go well with his cattle during the whole year, but the normal belief is that the four-leaved clover, on account of its cross form, is endowed with magical virtues. The general form of the superstition is that one who carries it about with him will be successful at play, and will be able to detect the proximity of evil spirits. In Bohemia it is said that if the maiden manages to put it into the shoe of her lover without knowledge when he is going on any journey, he will be sure to return to her faithfully and safely. In the Tyrol the lover puts it under the pillow to dream of the beloved.

On Christmas Eve, especially, one who has it may see witches. Plucked with a gloved hand and taken into the house of a lunatic without anyone else perceiving it, it is said to cure madness. In Ireland also it is deemed sacred and has been immortalized in Lover's beautiful song as a safeguard against every imaginable kind of sorrow and misfortune. It was a belief among the Jews, according to Zoroaster says Howitt, that every flower is appropriated to a particular angel, and that the hundred-leaved rose is consecrated to an archangel of the highest order. The same author relates that the Persian fire worshipers believe that Abraham was thrown into a furnace by Nimrod, and the flames forthwith turned into a bed of roses.

In contradistinction to this in sentiment is the belief of the Turk, who holds that this lovely flower springs from the perspiration of Mohammed, and, in accordance with this creed, they never tread upon it or suffer one to lie upon the ground. Of shrub or flower worship, the most important in the east and south has been that of the lily species. The lily of October- the saffron was very sacred to the Karnean, or horned Apollo- that is, the sun- for horns usually stand for rays of glory, as in the case of the horned Moses of our poets, artists and ecclesiastics, who make him like an Apis of Egypt, because of the text which says, 'his face shone' when he came down from the mountain. All lilies have more or less to do with the female or fecundating energies, and so even in Europe we have many stories of the crocus species, because it is said 'of their irradiating light, having peculiar looking bells, three-headed and crested capillaments, three cells, and reddish seeds,' etc.

FOLK MAGIC, SUPERSTITION, AND CHARMS

The Lotus is the seat of most deities, but notably so of the creator Brahma, who, thus enthroned, is called the Kamta-ayoni, or the great androgynous god. The lotus is the womb of all creation. It is said to originate from the great fertilizer, water, alone; and dropping its great leaves on this fertilizer as on a bed, it springs upwards with a slender, elegant stalk, and spreads forth in a lovely flower. Even the grave and mighty Vishnu delights in the lotus, which is one of the four emblems he holds in his fourfold arms. It is Venus' sacred flower." (p. 33-36.)

"The Lotos (Lotus) is held in the highest veneration in India, inclusive of Thibet and Nepaul. among the Brahmans and enthusiastic Hindus, no object in nature is looked on with more superstition; and their books abound in mystical allusions to this lovely aquatic. Being esteemed the most beautiful of vegetables, it not unappropriated furnishes a name for the Hindu queen of beauty, and Kamal or Kamala is a name of Lakshmi, as is Padma or Pedma, another Sanskrit appellation for both. Under the form of Kamala, Lakshmi is usually represented with a Lotos in her hand, and in most pictures and statues of her consort Vishnu, he is furnished with the Pedma, or Lotus bud, in one of his four bands, as a distinguishing attribute.

Accordingly, as it is represented in different stages of efflorescence, it varies, in the eyes of mystics, its emblematical allusions. As an aquatic, the Lotos is a symbol also of Vishnu, he being a personification of water or humidity, and he is often represented seated on it. Brahma the creative power, is also sometimes seated on the Lotos, and is borne on its calyx in the whimsical representation of the renovation of the world, when bottom of the sea where he was reposing on the serpent Lesha. Lakshmi, as we have just noticed, is the sakti or consort of Vishnu, the preservative power of the deity. The extensive sect of Vaishnava, or worshipers of Vishnu, esteem Lakshmi as mother of the world, and then call her Ada Maya; and such Vaishnavas as are saktas, that is, adorers of the supremacy of the female energy, worship her extensively as the type of the

Eternal Being, and endow her with suitable attributes. She is represented by the poets and painters as of perfect beauty. Hindu females are commonly named after her; and there are few in the long catalog of their deities whose various names and functions are so frequently alluded to in conversation and writing, either on theogony, mythology, poetry or philosophy." (p. 46-47.)

FLOWER LORE AND LEGEND
Katharine Beals, 1917

"Buttercup is the pet name for the bright little flower which Thoreau, the 'Hermit of Walden,' has called the 'gold of the meadow.' The family name of the flower is crowfoot, which, like most surnames, had its origin in something especially appropriate to the object named, as the leaves of the plant are shaped something like a crow's foot. The botanical name of the flower is ranunculus, the diminutive of rana, which means frog, and was given to it in the very ancient times because it so often grew in places where the frogs sing. Another reason for giving it the name is beautifully told by Herrick, the English poet. Ranunculus was a Libyan youth, who was noted for his melodious voice and his gorgeous attire. He dressed altogether in green and yellow silk, and sang so sweetly that every one who heard him was charmed. He himself would often forget that any one was listening to him. One day when he was singing to a group of wood nymphs, he became so entranced with his own music that he expired in ecstasy and Orpheus transformed him into the brilliant little flower that bears his name.

Tall crowfoot, one variety of buttercup, is supposed to be the plant referred to by Pliny as convivial, or the laughing leaves, which, when mixed with wine and myrrh and taken as a drink, caused strange visions to present themselves. It would excite the most inordinate laughter that often ended in death from convulsions. The only remedy he says for this singular condition was to dissolve pineapple kernels with pepper in wine from the date tree. It also has powerful caustic properties and it is said that if the leaves are bruised and applied to the skin, blisters, like those produced by the action of fire, will be raised. It was used by the ancients as a severe remedy in cases of leprosy and for removing birthmarks. Beggars sometimes resorted to it to produce sores upon their limbs to excite sympathy. The root was reputed to be a certain cure for insanity, if gathered at the wane of the moon, wrapped in a linen cloth, and suspended around the neck of the person affected. Feeding cattle avoid it. If they happen to get it, a blistered mouth is the result. (p. 54-55.)

"The forget-me-not, like the red-and-white rose, had its place in English history. When Henry of Lancaster was banished by Richard, he chose it for his emblem and the words, 'Couveigne vous de moi,' as his motto. They were woven into his knight's collar. His adherents, following his example, wore forget-me-nots as an evidence of their fidelity. One of these collars, made of gold with the flowers and motto enameled in blue, was given as a prize at a famous tournament, during the reign of Edward IV. It was won by Lord Scales, the brother of the Queen. More than one historian is authority for the fact that after the battle of Waterloo an immense quantity of forget-me-nots sprang up in different parts of the battlefield.

The Italians tell of a beautiful maiden who was beloved of the gods, and when she was drowned they transformed her into the blue forget-me-not, growing on the river bank. The name *myosotis* is derived from the Greek and signifies mouse-ear, because of the shape of the leaves. Another name by which the plant used to be called was scorpion grass, perhaps on account of the spike resembling the tail of a scorpion. It was popularly supposed to be a cure for the bite of that animal. Many flowers are assigned as appropriate to particular days. The day of the forget-me-not is February 29th.

In England, France, and the Netherlands, about the Middle Ages, the name forget-me-not was given to the ground pine on account of the bitter taste it leaves in the mouth, and in some parts of England it used to be called speed-well, because when the blossoms fell off they blew away. The name which was perpetuated by the ship that came to New England in the time of the Pilgrims is an ancient form of bidding farewell or good-by. There is hardly a poet who has not, at some time or other, taken the forget-me-not as a theme. Most of them use it in a sentimental fashion, but not all. Goethe calls it 'still the liveliest flower, the fairest of the fair.'" (p. 60-61.)

"The helianthus, or old-fashioned sunflower, is associated in the minds of almost every one with the ancient myth of Clytie and Apollo, as related by Ovid. The name is derived from *Helios*, the sun, and *anthos*, a flower, and there is no doubt that the sunflower in the minds of the Greeks bore a resemblance to the orb of the day. Some writers have endeavored to demonstrate that the heliotrope (one of the flowers sacred to the sun) was unknown to the ancients, so in lack of definite information the common mind has accepted, if not the sunflower of the present day, at least one of the same species as the subject of the legend.

One of the most familiar pieces of old sculptures discovered in modern times is the bust now in the British Museum and frequently reproduced, generally known as Clytie. The name was arbitrarily given to it because it rises from the leaves of a large blossom, which it does not require a vivid imagination to accept as a sunflower. Clytie was a beautiful water-nymph, the daughter of Oceanus. One day she left her home among the waves and the sea flowers and joined the assembly of the gods on Mount Olympus. There she saw Apollo, the sun-god, in all his glory, and, foolish little nymph, fell desperately in love with him. Apollo was just then very much enamored of Calliope, the muse of epic poetry, and paid no attention to Clytie. So she pined away, sitting all day long upon the cold ground, with her hair streaming on her shoulders, gazing upon the sun from the time he appeared in the morning until he sank behind the horizon. For nine days she sat there, tasting neither food nor drink, and resisting all entreaties of the other water-nymphs to return to her home in the sea. At last her limbs sank into the earth and became roots, her body changed into a long, slender stem, and her beautiful face was transformed into a flower, which reflected the rays of the sun and turned toward him all day in his course through the heavens. When the old-time Spanish invaders arrived in Peru they found that the worship of the sun still prevailed among the inhabitants and that the sunflower was much reverenced on account of its resemblance. They described the Temple of the Sun as ornamented with representations of the sun made of the purest gold and of exquisite workmanship.

The priestesses were crowned with sunflowers and wore them on their bosoms and carried them in their hands. Some of the travelers called the plant the Indian *sonne-fleur*; others the golden flower of Peru. It was introduced at that time into Spain. Within the next twenty years we find references made to the sunflower gardens of Madrid. As a symbol of constancy and devotion it has its place in the Christian religion. Being the flower of light and sunshine, it is dedicated to St. John the Evangelist. A window in the Church of St. Remi, at Rheims, represents the Holy Mother and St. John on either side of the Cross. The head of each is encircled by an aureole of sunflowers, all turned toward the Savior as to the true sun. An anonymous writer, in an ode to the sunflower, embodied this:

> 'Emblem of constancy, whilst he is beaming,
> For whom is thy passion so steadfast, so true;
> May we, who of faith and of love are aye dreaming,
> Be taught to remember this lesson by you.'"

(p. 74-76.)

"In Scotland it was once thought that one who had a four leaved clover on his person would immediately realize it if any one attempted to practice witchcraft upon him. Its virtue as a protection is referred to in these lines:

> 'With a four-leaved clover, double-topped ash, and
> green-topped seave,
> You may go before the queen's daughter without
> asking leave.'

This was accomplished by the combination. Seaves were the rushes from which the old rush lights were made. A reference to a different combination is also found in verse:

> 'An even-leaved ash,
> And a four-leaved clover,
> You'll see your true love,
> 'Fore the day is over.'

A four-leaved clover has long been supposed to invest the finder with great magical powers. Samuel Lover, in his Four leaved Shamrock, gives voice to the superstition:

> 'I'll seek a four-leaved shamrock, in all the fairy
> dells,
> And if I find the charmed leaves, oh, how I'll weave
> my spells.
> But I would play the enchanter's part in casting bliss
> around.
> Oh! not a tear or aching heart should in the world
> be found.'

The fairy folk, in olden times when there were fairies, appropriated the clover as one of their especial plants. Whenever a fairy foot touched the ground there came up a four-leaved clover, possessed of magical power. Whoever found one was immediately taken under the protection of the little people. If a maiden, she saw her true love before the day closed. If a youth, his success in his wooing was assured. If a lover went on a journey and his sweetheart put a four-leaved clover in his shoe, he had a safe return. The fortunate possessors of this talisman were the only mortals who could hold converse with the fairies when they wished. As it brought all sorts of good luck at play, it is said to have caused the club, which in France is called 'Trefle,' to have been placed on the playing cards." (p. 81-82.)

"There are few plants around which has gathered such a wealth of legend and tradition as has accumulated around the flower known as the mandrake. From the earliest times to which history takes us it was held in veneration by the inhabitants of the Eastern lands. Many of the superstitions associated with it are unpleasant and most of them are uncanny. The plant itself is insignificant. The leaves rise directly from the ground. They are sharp-pointed, hairy, and of a vivid, dark-green color. The flower is a sickly white, veined with purple. The root is long and shaped like a parsnip. It is often forked, causing fanciful persons to imagine that it bears some resemblance to a rudely formed human figure. To this fanciful likeness is due many of the superstitions that cluster around the plant. It was supposed by the Romans to be under the especial protection of Atropos, the sable-robed, grim-visaged fate, who remorselessly severed the thread of life which was spun by Clotho and twisted by Lachesis.

By the Greeks it was known as Circean and was dedicated to Circe, the daughter of the sun, the golden-haired enchantress, celebrated for her knowledge of witchcraft, who so nearly accomplished the undoing of those companions of Ulysses, when they accompanied him on his wanderings after the sacking of Troy back to Ithaca. The roots cling tenaciously to the earth, and it was a current superstition that whenever the plant was gathered it gave vent to terrible shrieks and groans that sounded almost human, and were said to cause instant death to any creature who heard them. As the plants held an important place as a medical remedy among the ancients, an ingenious, if rather inhuman, method of obtaining them was devised. The persons who gathered them, after carefully stopping their ears, fastened a dog securely to the plant by his tail. He was then driven or enticed away. Thus the root was dragged out of the earth, and the unfortunate animal dropped dead upon the spot as the plant emitted the most heart-rending screams.

An old Jewish writer is authority for this tradition, but it seems to have been widely current. Shakespeare makes several allusions to it. At a later period a belief seems to have prevailed that if gathered at holy times and with the repetition of certain invocations, which were probably anything but holy, the Evil One would aid the seeker of the plant, and it could be obtained with safety. Pliny writes that in Rome it was the custom of those who sought the roots to make three circles around the plant with the point of a sword, and then having turned toward the west they proceeded to dig it up. From ancient times, also, came the superstition that the plant grew only in dark places and thrived under the shadow of a gallows, near a gibbet, or where criminals were buried." (p. 115-116.)

"Verbena was an old Latin name for the flower that was later known throughout Europe as vervain. Both names mean a green bough. As an holy herb, it was held in the highest veneration by both Greeks and Romans, and marvelous qualities were attributed to it, not the least of which was the power of reconciling the bitterest enemies. It bore a prominent part in the official life of both nations. When the Romans felt that they had been treated discourteously by any of their neighbors, it was their custom to select four heralds from the members of the *fetiales*, whose duty it was to maintain the forms of international relationship, act as guardians of the public faith, and demand redress. These four selected one of their number to act as spokesman, who was sometimes the *pater patratus* or president of the college, but more generally he was merely a member and known as the verbenarius. Clothed in their priestly robes, wearing the insignia of their office, and preceded by the verbenarius, who in addition to his other vestments wore a white woolen band around his head, together with a wreath of the sacred verbena, gathered within the enclosure of the Capitoline Hill, and all bearing boughs of the same sacred plant, they advanced to the place where their negotiations were to be conducted. If war was decided upon, the verbenarius and his colleagues, wearing wreaths of verbena, approached the confines of the hostile territory. Throwing across the boundary a spear tipped with iron, and having a sprig of the holy herb bound upon its point, a solemn declaration of war was announced, and Jupiter was called upon to witness the justice of their cause. All treaties were approved by the college before they became effective and war was not declared until the demand for redress had first been made.

It was with water, in which this plant had been steeped, that the festal table of Jupiter was cleansed just before the feasts, which were prepared in the capitol by the septemviri in his honor. If the water was also used to sprinkle the banqueting couches before a feast, the merriment and hilarity was said to be thereby greatly promoted. Fletcher, in the Faithful Shepherdess, wrote:

> And those light vervain, too, thou must go after,
> Provoking easy souls to mirth and laughter.'"

(p. 129-130.)

"The rosemary may be called a versatile flower. It has been associated with life and death, with joy and sorrow. It has decorated with its luxuriant foliage the garden walls of proud Hampton Court, and has thrived in many a kitchen garden. It belongs to the mint family and was accorded a most honorable place among the ancients. The Latin calls it *rosamarius*, meaning dew of the sea, because it grows so luxuriantly near the seashore and also because the foliage has a silvery appearance as if covered with dew. It is said that the gray bushes along the rocky coasts of France and Italy well warrant the name. It was also called Mary's rose and was an emblem of the Virgin. The Greeks and Romans made garlands of it with which they crowned the guests of honor at their feasts. They also burned it as incense at many of their religious ceremonies. During the Palilia, or Shepherd's Festival, which was held in April to celebrate the founding of Rome by the shepherds and husbandmen, rosemary and laurel in large quantities were burned that the smoke might purify the sacred groves and fountains from unintentional pollution by the flocks and herds. It was one of the herbs used by the Romans in embalming their dead and its evergreen leaves symbolized to them the immortality of the soul. When they invaded Briton they brought with them many of their old rites and superstitions, and this may account for its popularity as a funeral emblem. Until comparatively recently in many parts of rural England it was strewn upon the coffin and sprays of rosemary were distributed to all those who attended the service that they might be cast into the grave as a final ceremony, emblematic of the life to come. One of the most pathetic incidents connected with the funeral of Princess Alice of Hesse was when a poor old peasant woman of the Odenwald timidly laid her little wreath of rosemary beside the rare and costly flowers that covered the casket. In spite of its association with the dead, as an emblem of memory and faithfulness the rosemary was in great demand as a bridal flower. Herrick refers to its double use when he said:

> 'Grow for two ends, it matters not at all,
> Be't for my bridal or my burial.'

It was customary for the bride to wear several sprays twined in her bridal wreath by some member of her family, to silently remind her to take with her to her new home memories of the dear old roof-tree and the loving hearts she was leaving behind. It was a token of gladness as well as of the dignity of the marriage sacrament. The bridal bed was decked with its sprays. The young men and maidens who attended the happy couple all wore or carried sprigs of rosemary, but it was to be borne in the heart as well as in the hand. Mystically it was thought to strengthen both the memory and the heart and to signify love and loyalty. In an old play is found the question: 'Was the rosemary dipped?' This refers to the custom of dipping a spray in the wine cup before drinking to the bridal couple." (p.181-182.)

FUNERAL CUSTOMS
Betram Puckle, 1919

"Various kinds of fir trees are also planted as recognized symbols of death; for unlike other trees, the life goes out of them directly they are cut. The cypress has held the place of honor throughout the ages, in connection with death. The Romans placed its branches in the vestibule as long as the body was there, to signify that it was a house of mourning, and it was also carried in the funeral procession. 'Rosemary,' says Ophelia, 'that's for remembrance,' and in comparatively recent times, the mourners held sprigs of box and rosemary at the burial, and deposited them on the coffin before leaving. Medicinally, rosemary was held to be good for improving the sight and the memory. The sprigs were arranged in a bowl on a table in the entrance hall of the house where the friends and relatives were assembled, to whom they were distributed.

In Japan, branches of sakaki are carried and used in part of the final ceremony- flowers also in abundance. We must not forget the palm, the symbol of victory over death, which the Christian festival of Palm Sunday reminds us was used at the 'entry into Jerusalem,' and which is associated by the Church with her martyrs. It is often to be found engraved on the Roman tombs. A very curious superstition is worth noting in connection with the mandrake, a plant similar to belladonna, and credited with having a personality, or if growing in a graveyard, attached to the spirit of the dead. There seems to be no better foundation for this belief than that it roughly resembled the human form, having two taproots of equal length which suggested the lower limbs. When pulled from the ground, the small fibers breaking, a sound is produced which was readily translated by the imaginative into a 'shriek.'

The Germans made the mandrake into dolls, dressing them with care and respect, and keeping them in caskets. Midnight was the correct time to dig them up, when all kinds of absurd rites were practiced, a 'black dog' being employed to drag them from the earth. Among other magical properties, they were supposed to be efficacious in the case of a barren woman, and are mentioned in the Bible in this connection. If trees have a close association with death, so too have flowers, and never more so than at the present time. The writer recently attended a funeral at which the value of the floral 'offerings' could not have been less than seventy or eighty pounds, and this is not anything very exceptional. The fact that white flowers are almost exclusively used for the purpose reminds us that they are a special token of purity. It was the practice of the Primitive Church to crown the heads of virgins with flowers. In Corsica, when a young girl dies, the body is dressed in her best clothes, the feet tied with a white silk ribbon (to prevent the spirit from wandering on earth) and her head crowned with a chaplet of flowers by her friends, who thus address her, 'We your companions, in bringing you lilies and roses, bring you your wedding garland.'

Besant mentions as a recent custom in Yorkshire, the hanging of a garland of flowers in the chancel of the church when a girl dies unmarried. The fact that the wreath was placed in the chancel, and that it was considered unlucky to carry away a piece of the ribbon with which the blossoms were tied, and the still more significant fact, that as the wreath decayed, the pieces were reverently buried in the churchyard, indicates that it was looked upon as an offering to the dead, rather than a sign of condolence with the living. Sometimes a white glove was attached to the wreath on which the name and age of the maiden would be inscribed. The white glove, like the white veil with which the Greek Church bury their dead women, has generally been used as a token of innocence. The white glove signifies a 'clean hand,' and it is still the custom to present a pair to the judge when there are no criminal charges to come before him, or, as at an earlier period, it was hoisted in the market-place on high days and holidays, a truce to those who were "wanted" for various crimes, who might venture forth from their hiding places to join in the festivities only as long as they were so protected. From what we have seen of the matter, it would seem that the funeral wreath of white flowers signifies virginal purity, and if this is so, we must admit that it is singularly out of place for general distribution." (p. 144-146.)

THE GRAND GRIMOIRE
1750

"SECTION III:

Containing the true composition of the mysterious or fulminating wand, as it is depicted here:

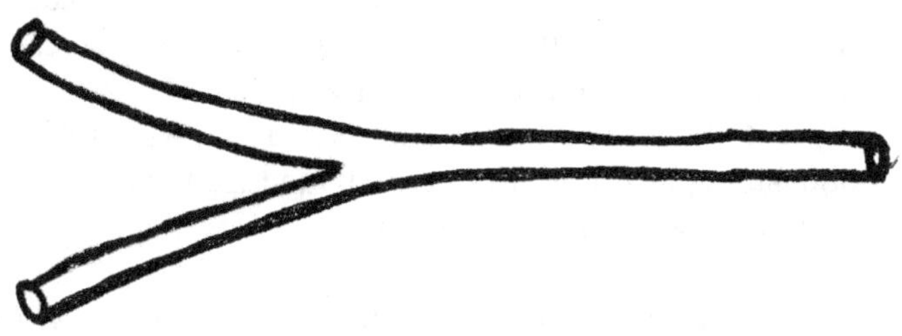

On the eve of the great undertaking you will search for a rod or wand of wild hazel tree that has not yet born fruit, at the highest point of the sought-after branch there should be a second little branch in the form of a fork with two ends; its length should be nineteen and a half inches. After having found a branch of this shape, only look at it but abstain from touching it, waiting for the following day, a day destined for action, in which you will go and cut it precisely at sunrise, and denude it of its leaves and small twigs, if there are any of these, and with the same blade that was used to skin the sacrifice, which will still be tainted with its blood; you will cut it when the sun starts to break forth on this hemisphere, pronouncing the following words:

'I beseech you, O great ADONAY, ELOHIM, ARIEL and JEHOVA to be favorable and to give this rod that I am cutting the strength of Jacob and the virtue of Moses and that of the great Joshua; and I beseech you, O great ADONAY, ELOHIM, ARIEL and JEHOVA to enclose in this rod all the power of Samson, the righteous rage of Emmanuel and the Thunderbolt of ZARIATNATMICK who will avenge man's affronts on the day of Judgment.'

After having pronounced these great and terrible words, always keeping your eyes turned toward the rising sun, cut the branch and take it to your room, then take a piece of wood that is of the same thickness as the two ends of the rod and take it to a Smith to cap the two ends of the fork with the steel blade that was used to skin the sacrifice, ensuring that the two blades are sharp and when they are fitted to the two pieces of wood, take them home, putting the two irons on the true rod yourself, then take a lodestone, heat it in the fire to magnetize the points of the rod pronouncing the following words:

'By the power of the great ADONAY, ELOHIM, ARIEL and JEHOVA, I beseech you to unite all of the materials that I desire by the power of the great ADONAY, ELOHIM, ARIEL and JEHOVA I command you by the incorruptibility of water and fire, to separate all of the materials as they were separated the day of the creation of the world. Amen.'

Following this I assure you (in the honor of the great ADONAY) being certain that you possess the greatest Treasure of the Light. The following evening take your rod, the kid skin, the Bloodstone, the two garlands of Verbena, then also, the two candle holders and two pounds of virgin wax that has been blessed; take also the lodestone and two smooth flint-stones to light the fire also half a bottle of Spirit of Water and a portion of blessed incense mixed with some camphor and four nails that were used in the coffin of a child who has recently died. Then take yourself to the place where you have to do the Great Work, doing exactly the following, executing point-by-point the great Kabbalistic Circle in the manner indicated." (p. 10-11.)

LIBER SALOMONIS
16th Century

"...And Raziel said, an herb shall be your life. And Solomon said, a tree shall in the future be that will grow and never cast off its leaves, and it shall be medicine of men.

The first herb is called rosemary. This herb is a small bush, with a fine fragrance, and little leaves and its power is to invigorate and clarify the brain. And if a house is fumigated with it, it chases demons away. The same also does the peony.

The second herb is artemesia and this is mother and first of the other. But because rosemary is sometimes called *Corona regis* that is to say the Crown of a king, we have put it first. Of this herb it is said that it should be included with all that you do, and whatever you wish shall come to pass. And the leaf is middle greenish on that one side and white on that other. And it is of middling size. And with this you may call or bind all spirits.

The third herb is cannabis and it is long in its stems and can be made into cloth. The virtue of the juice of cannabis is to anoint yourself with it, and stand before a mirror made of fine steel, and you can then call spirits forth into their images, and will see them visibly, and will be able to bind or call demons.

The fourth herb is called carrot and it has a long stem and small leaves. And it is an holy herb and worshipful. And it is medicine of the eyes and keeps evil spirits at bay, repelling evil even where it grows. The root of it chases away many evil things and aids the sight.

The fifth herb is cardamom and it is hot and of good complexion, and it is of middling height and gives gladness to him that uses it. It can gather together spirits. Eat of this when you perform invocations, and if you do you will succeed.

The sixth herb is anise and it is of chastity joined to camphor and it causes spirits to fear you. And it is a clean herb and it makes one to see secret things and be privy to them. The fume of this ascends much.

The seventh herb is coriander, and this causes a man to lose his vigor and fall into a deep sleep if it is wished. And this gathers spirits together as well. Wherefore evermore they stand with it, so that it is said that if a fumigation is made from coriander and celery it will gather all spirits together at once.

The eighth herb is called sage which has great ability to chase insects away. And its virtue is to break the stone in the bladder of him that uses it.

The ninth herb is hypericon and it is an herb of middling size, with a sap which appears like blood. This is of great power for if one takes the juice mixed with croco and artemesia and with the fume of valerian if it be written upon what friendship you wish, of a Prince of Spirits of the Air and devils both know that it will be as you have declared. It will empower you over all spirits of the air.

The tenth herb is parsley. This is of great power upon winds and devils, and fantasies, and it is shaded and touched to shade and the clouds always are over it for in it is the power over all such spirits. They be much contrary for one is kept with the angels and another with demons. And this breaks the stone of the kidneys. And a woman with child should not use it for it may harm the child. And it gathers together demons when it is used to fumigate, and the fume is made with it added to artemesia, using it for seven nights subsequently, gathered cleanly and the root of it dried and prepared with *aqua lapidis*. Suffume your home and you shall see the devils and spirits for yourself.

The eleventh herb is a second kind of coriandrum, the kind which causes all to fall asleep. And you may make incense of the same mixed with croco, mixed together as well evenly and tempered with citrus juice and musk. And then suffume the place where you will hide treasure, when the moon and sun are joined in the skies. Know that this treasure will never be found, and if anyone should stumble upon and disturb it it they will be struck dumb. And in the hour of deposition of the gold or silver of the stones or images that you are making, use an incense made with thur, musk, citrus, and aloe wood, and this same coriandrum, and evermore devils will keep that place with their evil winds. And know that it might never be dissolved or found out without Semiphoras or an image made thereto by the point of the stars.

The twelfth herb is satureja, this is of great virtue and of good odor, and whoever that bears it with him with *arrucila muris* in the day of Venus, it gives the grace of heaven and takes affliction from them.

The thirteenth herb is that which is called hyssop and this is middling in height with small leaves: this ought to be grown with reverence in holy places as in churches for it defends the place from evil things. And it was grown by the prophets which made dead men to speak that were dead for some time. In places where is any evil he that bears this herb is able to pass freely. And it gives to him might upon anything which he wishes. And this herb can be placed in an area overrun with evil and will bind the same. And Solomon said, I found in the book of Hermes, that who that takes water in the fourth hour of the night and goes upon the tomb of a dead man with and mixes this herb into the water and casts it on the tomb may communicate with the spirit therein. And the water should be mixed with the juices of the same and the person shall say 'rise, rise, rise, come and speak to me.' And do this for three nights and in the third he shall come to you and speak about what you wish.

The fourteenth herb is psyllium which is of great virtue: for it causes the weather to become fair when used. And it makes one to see spirits in the clouds of the skies. And this may be mixed with chicory and garmone, and the tree which is called the tree of cancer, and with the tree that blossoms by night, which it is called *herba lucens,* that is, the shining herb. If you make with these an ointment with the eye of a whelp and with the heart fat of the same, you may use the same to travel at incredible speed.

The fifteenth herb is marjoram, and this keeps a house safe, especially from sickness. And Hermes said that gentian, valerian, and marjoram avail much upon great honor of princes and of great men.

The sixteenth herb is tarragon. This is of great power and the it may be mixed with a snake's tongue to cause bleeding. And the herb should be gathered when the sun is in Cancer, and the moon is in Mercury, or is in the house of Mercury, or joined with him. Know that the bearer can cause anyone to befriend them. And Hermes said that it gathers together winds and spirits if mandrake is added to it in an ointment.

The seventeenth herb is catnip. This with marjoram, athanasia, clover, sage, peruca, ivy, artemesia and hyssop are all joined together under a crescent Moon with Jupiter, that is to say in the waxing of the Moon on Jupiter's day, in the morrow when the sun rises from the first degree of Aries till into the first of Cancer. And when you gather the same be clean and reverent, then stand toward the East. Know that the house and the place is amended where these herbs were joined together and put them upon the gate of your house and you will profit forever.

The eighteenth herb is linseed. A fumigation of the same made with parsley can make one see the future among other things.

The nineteenth herb is salvia. This is of great virtue and the long leaf of it is like a sharp tongue. The plant repels all evil from wherever it is grown. And it is good for a man to bear salvia with him, for it holds a man whole and well, but it will not profit a sick man.

The twentieth herb is samina. And some say that it is a tree. This is a tree of love and dedication, for those who may find it. And if this is mixed with some croco and with the tongue of a bird and be born with a man in a ring of gold with some provinca, and you can surely go before the king or before whomever you must, and prosper. And put this with topaz or beryl as well if you wish. And if this ring is made when the Moon is joined to Jupiter in triune to the Sun it is much the better. And it is called *Annulus Solis* that is the Ring of the Sun and it is of health and against sickness, it is of grace and virtue and much honor.

The twenty first herb is nasturtium. This holds the members whole and one may mix with it oregano, pulegium, and fern and if it be borne together with you and you eat them, you will retain your health. And so the same if you anoint yourself with them, and if you are fumigated with horehound, albofor, barberry, and scilla, it shall defend against all sickness.

The twenty second is an herb that it called canna. This is dreadful and powerful. And if you take its juice with the juice of citrus and alchemilla, with sandalwood and false hellebore and perfume yourself with this you can see many odd things. And if Artemisium is mixed with this know that from each place thus fumigated, devils will flee. This fumigation is evil and horrible. Both the vapor of the same and the workings with this are evil. And more strongly this is so if the Moon were with Saturn or in opposition with Mars.

The twenty third herb is calamus and it is likened to mint and it is of great virtue in good perfumes. If palm and mint are added to the same, then these be will protect a place against evil.

The twenty fourth herb is chicory. This is fully good herb in all exorcisms and it should be joined with eryngium and pentaphylum and hypericon and vertica and verbena, and all be together on the neck and underfoot. As well, let there be the seven knots and seven leaves of martagon lily, domesticated lily, and gymnema, that is tame and wild thus mixed with *herba angelica.* Whoever has these under the feet or sits on them, and wears seven rings of seven metals on the fingers, may do any good or evil, enchant or disenchant, and be protected wherever the herbs have been burned. Also make a perfume with the following: thur, albo, fumitory, mastic, musk, wood aloe, cassia, cinnamon. And if you fumigate the area with the same, then say these names: '*Raphael, Gabriel, Michael, Cherubin, Seraphin, Arrielim, Pantaseron, Micraton, Sandalon- fulfill ye my petition and my will*' and they should fulfill it to you. And these be the names of the nine angels aforementioned. And know these and remember them. And some say these are also the nine orders of the angels." (p. 35-42.)

MYTHS AND LEGENDS OF FLOWERS, TREES, FRUITS, AND PLANTS
Charles Skinner, 1911

"Plants of Ill Renown

There was once in the middle of Java a certain tree that dripped and breathed poison, destroying animal and vegetable life for miles around. Even the birds fell dead when flying past. It stood alone in a valley which it filled with vapors, and all about it the earth was covered with the skeletons of men and animals that had strayed into the neighborhood. This famous upas tree (upas is Malay for poison) was the only one in existence, but the name is still applied to a tree of the same order as the breadfruit and mulberry. Its juices, mixed with pepper and ginger, are smeared upon arrows to make them irritating, and its bark yields a fiber used in native cloth which will cause itching unless it is soundly washed before wearing. On so slight a basis was the legend of the upas reared. Allied to the dreadful tree of Java is the rattlesnake bush of Mexico, with its venomous thorns.

From this arose a story of a tree of serpents that wound its arms about men and animals that tried to pass, and stung and strangled them to death. Nearly as vexatious is the kerzra flower, of Persia, for if you so much as breathe the air that has passed over it you must die. Nor is the manchineel an object of fond regard, inasmuch as death comes to any that shall rest beneath its branches and suffer themselves to sink into the sleep that its exhalations will induce. Trees usually bring luck to their owners, but the walnut is an exception. It is thought to kill vegetation near it, and to bear especial enmity to the oak. Paschal II hewed down a walnut in Rome because he discovered that the evil soul of Nero was living in its branches, and after the destruction of the tree the Church of the People was built upon its site as a security against the demon. Thus it appears that the wakiut is hospitable to wicked spirits. By some similar token, the yew was long thought to be dangerous to life and health, although thousands of men made bows from its wood and carried them without hurt except to other people. While the powers of good control various of the plants, others are under spell of evil creatures who work their will by poisons, but who also show themselves to those they would afflict. Belladonna is so beloved of the Devil that he goes about trimming and tending it in his not abundant leisure. He can be diverted from its care on only one night in the year, and that is Walpurgis, when he is preparing for the witches' sabbat. If on that night a farmer looses a black hen the Devil will chase it, and the watchful farmer, suddenly darting on the plant, may pluck and put the weed to its rightful use; for by rubbing his horse with it the animal gains strength, provided the herb is gained in the way here indicated. The apples of Sodom are held to be related to this plant, and the name belladonna, or beautiful lady, records an old superstition that at certain times it takes the form of an enchantress of exceeding loveliness, whom it is dangerous to look upon.

We may dismiss as mythical the traveled tale of a Venus fly-trap which was magnified into quite another matter before Captain Arkright was through with it, for such tales grow larger the farther they go from their beginning. It was in 1581 that the valiant explorer learned of an atoll in the South Pacific that one might not visit, save on peril of his life, for this coral ring enclosed a group of islets on one of which the Death Flower grew; hence it was named El Banoor, or Island of Death. This flower was so large that a man might enter it- a cave of color and perfume- but if he did so it was the last of him, for, lulled by its strange fragrance, he reclined on its lower petals and fell into the sleep from which there is no waking. Then, as if to guard his slumber, the flower slowly folded its petals about him. The fragrance increased and burning acid was distilled from its calyx, but of all hurt the victim was unconscious, and so passing into death through splendid dreams, he gave his body to the plant for food. Dreads such as are recorded in this narrative extended to the humblest forms of vegetation, and our uncanny fungi have not escaped the ascription of many evils. True, their reputation for poisoning is in part deserved, though there are more beneficent mushrooms than mischievous, and, as Hamilton Gibson proved, hundreds of tons of wholesome food go to daily waste in our fields for lack of knowledge among the people to recognize the edible varieties or to know when to gather and how to cook them. The common puffball is ripe for the kitchen while it is in its white state, for instance, but is past eating when it has turned leathery and throws out its gust of 'smoke' or spores when trodden. A giant puff-ball is reported which held food for at least one family, inasmuch as it weighed forty-seven pounds and was three feet thick! It is the threads of old puff-balls that supplied our grandfathers with tinder in the days when fire was started with flint and steel, and their dust was also used to stop blood flow, as some use cobwebs in emergencies today. Punk, in use on our Fourth of July, is also made from fungus. In parts of England the puff-ball is Puck's stool and Puck's fists, and some etymologists identify Puck with pogge, or toad.

Why are toadstools so named? Surely none ever saw a toad seated on one of them. The stools are apt to be kicked to pieces by the peasantry, especially if they are found growing in pixie rings, for then they surely shelter elves; and if an elf peers at you then quinine should be taken, for you are 'due to come down with fever.' If it is a cow that is looked at by the elf, she is thenceforth bewitched, and will give sour milk, or discover a disposition to dance and turn somersaults. These pixie rings are merely growths spreading centrifugally and sometimes overlapping. As grass inside the rings is shadowed by the fungi and loses a measure of its sustenance to them, the country folk ascribe the bare appearance of the sod to the dancing of the elves. The rings disappear in three or four years, and then it is said that the fairies have taken offense and gone elsewhere. The spores dropping from the parent plant exhaust the soil as they take root, and for that reason the growth is outward, not inward, the circles constantly widening toward new feeding grounds. The low form of life known as lichen spreads in a similar manner. It is the purple streaks on its stem rather than the scathe in its juice that gives a bad name to water hemlock- the plant that put Socrates to death- for these streaks are copies of the brand put on Cain's brow when he had committed murder. The plant bears the names of spotted cowbane, musquash root and beaver poison, in America, and is related to carrot, parsnip, parsley, fennel, caraway, celery, coriander, and sweet cicely, the latter also unwholesome. Jack-in-the-pulpit, or Indian turnip, known in England as lords-and-ladies, is another plant from which it was wise to keep a distance. Its name, *ariscema triphyllum*, signifies bloody arum, because its spathe is purple where Christ's blood fell upon it at the crucifixion. In our own country the laurel or kalmia was regarded with such dislike that people were warned against eating the flesh of birds that had fed on its berries. Even worse than laurel is the savin, called likewise magician's cypress and devil's tree, because it was used by wizards in some of their most sinful ceremonies. Our common milkwort, *polygala vulgaris*, is beneficent, and increases the milk of mothers who carry it in procession or wear it as a garland in Rogation week; but the Javanese variety, *polygala venanta*, is a dreadful herb, inasmuch as the native who touches it must sneeze himself to death.

Another plant of fell property is the garget or poke, although its young shoots are boiled and eaten like asparagus, and its tincture is administered for rheumatism by granny doctors. The catalog of roadside mischiefs would be incomplete without the henbane- bane of hens- or hog's bean, whose scientific mask is hyoscyamus, and which is held to be of so evil an aspect, with its woolly leaves and unsanctified-looking flowers, that one hardly needs to be warned from it. Witches use this in their midnight stews, and the dead in hades are crowned with it as they wander hopelessly beside the Styx." (p. 22-25.)

"Ash

The name 'ash' was derived from the Norse aska, meaning man, for it was from a twig of this tree, crooked like an arm, that Odin fashioned the first of our race. Achilles used an ashen spear, and Cupid made his arrows of the wood. The clubs of early warfare were often of ash, for its wood is tough and lasting. Its names of 'husbandman's tree' and 'martial ash' indicate its importance in the industries and arts of battle. Pliny, in his unnatural natural history, assures us that evil creatures have a dread of it, and that a serpent will cross fire rather than pass over its leaves. English mothers would rig little hammocks to ash trees where their children might sleep while field work was going on, believing the wood and leaves to be a protection against dangerous animals and more dangerous spirits. A bunch of the leaves guarded any bed from harm, and that house which was surrounded by an ash grove was secure indeed. 'May your footfall be by an ash's root,' is an old English form of wishing luck. The Germans gave honey from the ash to the new-born babe, just as the Scottish Highlanders give a drop of its sap to the infant as his first food. During Yule-tide festivals the ashen log was burned, and the ashen fagot carried the sacred fire from the old year to the new. In England the burning of ashen logs and fagots at Christmas was the gladdest occasion of the year, and the first withe that broke in the fire indicated the early marriage of the girl who had chosen it.

In Scandish legend, the foundation of the world was the sacred ash Yggdrasil, which sprang from the void, ran through the earth (a disk with a heavenly mountain in the center), and threw its branches into the higher heavens. Its leaves were clouds, its fruits the stars. Its three roots delved into hell, or Hela's realm, where, before the creation, was no light, no life. At each root gushed a spring- the spring of force, the spring of memory, the spring of life. Beside the main stem were the wells, that of Mimir in the north, from which the ocean flows; and that in the cheery south, where the waters of Urdar spread, with swimming swans that symbolize the sun and moon. Says the Voluspa: 'An ash I know called Yggdrasil, high and refreshed by purest water that comes back in dew, it stands ever green over Urdar.' Midgard, or the world, was attached half way up the trunk and supported by the branches. Outside of the habitable land stretched the ocean, and on the earth's extreme rim, lying on the surface of the sea, lay the serpent, its tail in its mouth as it encircles the world, symbolizing continuity and eternity. Still outside the ocean were mountains forming a barrier to any adventurous foot that might wander so far. On the fruit of the tree, which Iduna, goddess of life, threw down to them, the gods lived and increased in strength, though other forms of the legend say that the fruit was not ash-berries, but apples. Three sisters, or norns, representing the past, present, and future, kept the tree flourishing with melted snow from the northern hills. Other Norse legends are associated with Yggdrasil:

Odin's leaving his eye to Mimir as a pledge means only that the light of his eye was darkened when the sun sank every evening in the sea- when he descended to learn wisdom of the dwarf. The life-giving mead that Mimir drank every morning was the daybreak. The fourth day of the fourth week was Ash Odinsday, or Wodensday. And every year the people were taught of Yggdrasil by the priests; how its life pervaded all lesser things, making of men who shared it the relatives of beasts and even of the trees; how beneath the tree is hid the gjallarhorn that shall sound over the world when comes the twilight of the gods, or day of judgment; how on that day Yggdrasil will bow, the sea rush foaming over the land, heaven open, and the fire spirits leap from below, spreading ruin everywhere. Yet after the destruction Yggdrasil shall grow again, larger and more beautiful than before, the gods will reassemble, men shall live, and the chain of being will be carried higher than it has yet reached. There is a little tree known as the sorb, roan, rowan, or mountain ash, that saved the life of Thor when he was swept away by a flood in the Vimur. Feeling himself lifted from his feet in the current, he laid hold on the tree, and so came into vogue the saying, 'The sorb is Thor's salvation.' For a long time after the North was nominally converted, it was still the custom for ship-builders to put at least one plank of sorb into the hull of every ship, in the belief that Thor would look after his own. The Scottish Highlanders put a cross of rowan over their doors in order to keep their cows in milk, for no witch would enter where this cross was placed. To make the cattle doubly safe, hoops of rowan were fashioned that the cows might be driven through them on the way to stable. Good fairies are kind to children who carry rowan berries in their pockets, for these berries may at one time have been prayer beads, the occurrence of the ash near Druid monuments giving rise to a belief that it was sacred in more than one faith. In Iceland, the tree springs from the graves of innocent persons who have been put to death, and lights will shine among its branches; yet it is a mischievous thing, for whereas Thor's plank will save a Norwegian ship, it will sink one made in Iceland; it will destroy a house, moreover, and if buried on the hearth will estrange the friends who sit around it.

The variety of ash called the service tree, which is related to the shad bush of this country, has edible berries, and yields an intoxicating beverage. As the spirit of this tree watches cattle, a Finnish shepherd will sometimes plant a stick of it in his pasture, when offering prayers for the protection of his stock." (p. 43-46.)

"*Fir*

The fir, which has been a sacred tree ever since it was hewn for the ceiling of the Temple at Jerusalem, was Atys- he whom Zeus changed to a tree, that he might thus appease the anger of Cybele, for Atys, a priest of Cybele, had lapsed from virtue: hence his punishment. So strong was the regard for the tree in France that when St. Martin arrived and began to raze the temple erected to heathen gods, his proposition to destroy the firs roused such anger that he was forced to desist. Some remains of its heathen association linger in the Hartz, where girls dance about it in their religious festivals, singing songs that are not Christian, and decorating it with lights, flowers, eggs, and gewgaws. In circling about it thus, they prevent the escape of an imp concealed among its branches, who must give to them whatever is in his keeping or resign hope of going free. This is held to be the origin of the Christmas tree, and the imp has grown to the benevolent St. Nicholas, Santa Claus, or Old Nick, who is believed by Grimm and other students of folk-lore to be no other than Odin himself. Christianized somewhat out of likeness. When you light up the tree on Christmas eve, making sure it is a fir and not a pine or spruce or hemlock, for we use all sorts of evergreens in our celebration, you may learn your fate, if you have courage to look at your shadow on the wall. If the shadow appears without a head, it signifies that you are to die within the coming year. If you will cut off a branch and lay it across the foot of your bed, it will keep away nightmare. A stick of fir, not quite burned through, fends off lightning, and a bunch hung at the barn door keeps out evil spirits that want to steal the grain. In Christmas celebrations in the neighborhood of the hill in the Hartz mountains known as the Hubinchenstein, cones gathered from the firs growing thereon are silvered and used for ornament, and if you ask why, you learn that long ago, when a miner fell sick, leaving his wife and children in straits for food and fuel, the wife climbed the Hubinchenstein, intending to pick up cones, which she might possibly sell for another day's living. As she entered the wood, a little old man with a jolly face and long white beard emerged from the shadows and pointed to a fir tree that he said would yield the best seeds. The woman thanked him, and when she reached the tree there was such a downfall of cones that she was frightened. The basket was extraordinarily heavy, too; indeed, she could barely reach her home with it, and the reason for this was soon evident, for when she emptied the cones upon the table, every one was of silver.

In the northern countries respect for the fir, as king of the forest and home of the wood genius, is so genuine that some choppers refuse to cut it, and when a monster fir is thrown down by storm in Russia the wood is not sold, but is given to the church." (p. 97-98.)

NATURE WORSHIP
Hargrave(?) 1891

"The branch of palm has now taken its place in the imagery of heaven and the typology of the eternal. In the Book of Revelation those who stand before the throne are portrayed with palms in their hands. Horus is represented in the monuments as defending himself against his evil enemy, Sut, or Satan, with a palm-branch in his hand. The branch of palm was, and still is an emblem of renewal. But the branch of birch that was buried with the dead in the barrows had the same meaning. A barrow at Kepwick was found to be lined with the bark and branches of the birch. That is the Bedmen of the British, which was also the maypole and the phallus. The Bedmen was typical of the resurrection equally with the palm." (p. 33-34.)

PLANTING, HARVESTING, AND SURGICAL OPERATIONS ETC ACCORDING TO THE SIGNS OF THE ZODIAC
Prof. A.F Seward, 1920

"Growing Sweet Melons

Obtain any species of sweet melon seed, and let it steep for two days in a syrup which will consist of raspberries, cinnamon, cardamom, two grains of musk and ambergris finely ground. The syrup must not be thick and warm when you put it in the seed infusion; now sow it over a layer of horse manure, and have great care not to over-water the plants and hope to avoid also the excessive rains. If done properly, this yields melons fit for royalty."

FOLK MAGIC, SUPERSTITION, AND CHARMS

"Growing Good Grapes

You have to have a cherry tree that is planted against a wall or trellis, with good sun exposure and good soil, and have a skilled gardener plant a couple of good vine stocks on said cherry tree, doing so in spring or late winter. Spare no good manure or watering and the grapes will be marvelous when they are mature.

To Prosper At Growing Wheat

You will need a pound of salts, composed of sulfur, niter, and saltpeter. Good druggists have this salt. Place this in six quarts of boiling water with two new books of good wheat seed, until the wheat seed begins to shrink and die, and then you will pass this composition through clear water; after this you will infuse into the cooled mix as much as you can of good wheat seed for twenty-four hours, your field already prepared. Sow this wheat seed thus infused and having dried the composition. Til and furrow the land and you will see by experience that the wheat you'll have sown will produce twenty times more than common wheat: it is true that we should not do that twice in the same land; because it will destroy the soil.

To Prevent Animals From Destroying Your Crops

You will need ten large crayfish, which you put in a vessel filled with water, and expose them to the sun for ten days. Now broadcast the water for eight days while sowing; and when it is done, sprinkle whatever is left, and you will see that the fields are clean of rats and other pests.

To Divine Whether Next Year's Planting Will Be Good

Zoroaster himself gives an infallible secret to know the abundance of the harvest for the following year. It takes about two days, in June, to perform. Prepare a small dirt patch, like we ordinarily ready to be planted, and now, sow all manner of seed in this, and because that in this season heat is hot and could affect what seeds are sown and which are more convenient to sow as well. After that you will see which seeds thrive and which do not, and will see which have the best appearance in time as the heat begins to reign over the horizon; as you will be notified by this test which seeds prosper and which die or produce little. So the wise farmer will take it on its measures for an abundant harvest.

Another Method

You shall see in the spring in what state the walnuts are: for if they appear loaded with foliage and few flowers, rest assured that nature will be stingy in the distribution of its wealth; if instead you see abundance of flowers on the nut trees, and the amount exceeds that of the leaves, fertility is assured: the almond tree performs similarly." (p. 36-38.)

"What to Plant and When to Plant It

Every man that tills the soil is at work in God's laboratory. He is to bring together all of the opportunities, the seed, the proper state of the soil and at the opportune moment place them for the Creator's law to begin the operation. The chemist will produce ice in a red hot crucible and place it before you, but ignorance cannot do this or a thousand other scientific things. The common ignorant laborer can make mortar but much of it is ruined in the process.

Then first let us learn when to put the seed in the ground and having prepared the ground let us know that Cancer is the very best sign for nearly everything grown. And here we may as well learn of Cancer. It is the sign governed by the Moon and rejoices therein; as the Moon governs the tides it has certainly great power over the water, and as water is the element that carries nearly everything in solution, it is the great factor in nearly all the chemical changes that take place on Earth. You will begin to see that moisture then takes up in solution the elements you require in every straw, stalk or stem you raise, but it does not move without help. There must be energy behind it, and this is provided in electricity. This sign above all others produces a much slighter vine or stem, a more lovely green, yet tender and as effeminate as a maiden. It is like the delicate, pale mothers that bear an abundance of children; so it is a fruitful sign, the strength going to seed, grain or fruit. Its great effect is to reproduce- hence it loads itself with fruit at the expense of the stalk.

It is movable, the germs are active on the slightest opportunity and grow up with the greatest energy. Potatoes, beets, radishes and all Garden Vegetables should be planted when the Moon is in the Signs of Cancer, Scorpio, Pisces and Taurus. For lettuce, beans, corn, wheat, rye and barley plant when the Moon is in the Signs of Cancer and Libra. For full pulp or foliage growth such as corn, fodder, alfalfa, millet, cabbage, celery and peas plant when the Moon is in the Sign of Libra, or Capricorn, but it should be remembered that Cancer and Scorpio are good for everything. Celery should always be planted when the Moon is in Libra as it will then grow quickly.

The next best sign in the order given is Scorpio, which is governed by Mars and must not be called effeminate, as Mars is one of the principal factors in the wars, and pertains to Are and iron, surgery, cutlery, etc. It produces quick germination, rapid growth, and an abundant fruitage, grain or seed. Pisces is next in order of quantity, because it falls always in the old of the Moon in the northern hemisphere, yet in some respects it is a better sign than Scorpio, and might rank second instead of third. Pisces is governed by Jupiter, which is of great influence. It is the greatest factor of all the planets in its electric manipulations, being fruitful and watery, producing fruit, enduring the drought next to Cancer, being an abundant producer, and like Scorpio produces less stalk and more grain. The next best sign is Libra, which is governed by Venus, and this planet pertains to women. Seed sown when the moon is in this sign germinates quickly, grows rapidly and strong and tenaciously; will have a strong, deep, rich, green color, and will grow more to stalk than grain, yet will yield a fair crop of grain, but is better for such fodder as may be desired to grow quickly, large and succulent, and is especially good for roots, particularly all roots that produce their seed the second year or biennially. The tendency of this sign is to pulp growth, and meadows produce hay and follow with fine pasture, and endure the trampling of cattle without apparent injury. Rye pastures will finally recover and produce a crop of grain. Venus is a moist planet, and when in combination with the Moon produces clouds or rain, and bestows her loving care to all plants placed under her control.

Libra is not considered Fruitful but is used for seeding hay, grain, fodder, etc. Many use it for Lettuce, Cabbage, and vegetables of quick growth, leaves and foliage above the ground but it is not as good as Taurus for this purpose.

Next in the list of productive signs is Capricorn, which is a cool, moist and movable sign, producing quick germination and rapid growth. Like Venus it produces strong, vigorous plant growths, and is best for fodder pasture, all roots and pulp growth and a fair crop of grain. Aries is considered a good sign, as it is a movable sign. It is governed by Mars, but always during the planting season is in the old of the Moon and is not much used. In latitudes south, when early spring makes it possible to use Aries in February or March, it should be considered like Libra or Capricorn.

Taurus is an earthly sign governed by Venus, and is considered to be a good sign, as it can be used in early spring. We describe it: It is good for potatoes and most crops having the good office of Venus' kindly care. Yet it is so little used, its real standing among the signs is not well understood, except that it is good; yet there are so many arguments pro and con on such early tests that we place it fairly before the reader for his test. The early market gardeners And it a good sign.

All of the above signs described are of that prolific quality that produce an abundance of chlorophyll, constant in abundance, keeping in advance of the organizing effect of the light and rays of the Sun upon the green in the leaves, which reduce the inorganic matter raised by electric energy in the fluid state, thus producing an abundance of the fat, plump desired condition of the crop so earnestly sought after in every crop that is raised.

The sign Leo is governed by the Sun. Under this sign the reproductive qualities are wanting, and the quality of the Sun being to organize the liquids brought up and placed in the form of chlorophyll into organic matter, hence that process goes on so rapid that the little that it does acquire is readily hardened into solids to the hindrance of other like supplies being sent up. There is apparently but very little growth, and that of such a hard and woody substance, it is of little or no value; in fact, there is but little supply, and in most cases they are subject to the attack of insects and never make more than a slight effort, and soon give up the effort.

Gemini is the poorest sign for the production of grain or almost any of the crops usually produced. It is a barren sign like Leo. It is governed by Mercury which pertains to the brain. Countries ruled by this sign are quick, active people, mentally and physically, and as a rule crops under this sign will produce more straw or stalks, but it will be very light in grain, and like Leo it is the best for destroying noxious growths, especially in those days when occupied by the Moon.

Virgo comes third in rank as a barren sign. It is also governed by Mercury, but has a redeeming quality of being an earthy sign and with a favorable season and a favorable ingress will sometimes produce a fair crop, but more often it produces disappointment and failure.

Sagittarius is governed by Jupiter. The first half of the sign is productive, the last half is not so- rather an indifferent sign.

Aquarius is governed by Uranus and is rather an indifferent sign, better for destroying noxious growths. In connection with all this it becomes as necessary to know why and for what purpose you cultivate the crop, and as we work and read to do our work just right, and to love the work because we do know it, brings us pleasure. We cultivate first to give free circulation of moisture; second a free circulation of air, but above all as electricity loves moisture and the air, it is to give free exchange to the negatives of the Earth and the positive electricity of the air, as it is electricity that does the work, and the moisture of earth and the air are the mediums through which electricity can act upon the plants. The few inches of the surface of the earth is the field in which, like the bees of the hive, the great industry of moisture goes on. Air and electricity are tumbling over each other in that fond embrace never dreamed of by mortal man.

The slight crust formed on the surface of a cultivated field by the fresh breeze will in a few hours after a shower cut off almost entirely this free intercharge of the electric currents, which at this very time above all others is or should be doing its finest work and should be courted with the greatest zeal. Here then is your great fertilizer, awaits your call, stands at your door begging you to be taken in, then you will see the necessity of stirring the ground as soon after a smart shower as the ground will remain loose ; and stir it often to bring new earth in contact or in touch with your loving friend who is ready to do so much for you. To kill the weeds is a small part of the object, but incidentally see that they do not take the attention of your friend from the labors he is performing for you. We have seen in wheat, where it has grown rapidly, then slackened, and the organization of the chlorophyll which has been brought well up by the Sun, so that the stalk is a well developed organic substance, that a new Moon, a good rain, air full of vapor, warm and sultry, sends up such an abundance of inorganic matter through stalk so organized as to nearly shut off the flow of the fluid; it bursts the straw and the result is a waste of the material that should have gone to the grain, resulting in shrunken grain and corroded stalk, called rust This rust is the mineral or chemical substance held in solution by the water, which evaporates, leaving the inorganic substance in its native state, which again is oxidized by the same kindly agent, taken up again in solution to be lifted to the next plant or deposited in the earth by drought, and again taken up and carried on, to be caught by some industrious toiling son of man.

Cancer is the best sign for nearly all crops except those specially noticed as best under other signs; as it is a fruitful, movable and watery sign under which its plants endure successfully severe drought. It is especially good for all grain, clover or timothy and red top for seed, beans, peas, all vines, like cucumbers, squash, melons, etc., lettuce, cabbage and all fruits.

Scorpio and Pisces are next in value and good for the same purposes, also potatoes.

Libra and Capricorn are good for all roots, carrots, parsnips, beets, turnips, rutabagas, radishes and the like; all pulp growth, clover and grass for hay or pasture.

Taurus is probably next in value and all the crops do reasonably well under this sign, especially potatoes.

Aries is like Libra and Capricorn but not as favorably situated to be of much use in the northern hemisphere; but in the southern hemisphere it is of more use.

Leo, Gemini and Virgo are the best in the order given for destroying noxious growths, when occupied by the Moon.

So is Sagittarius and Aquarius and the old of the moon as they readily are destroyed at these times.

Let constant cultivation be the rule before noxious plants can get a footing; and the old of the moon and Moon in Leo is the time to kill Canada thistles, willows and all the tenacious shrubs. Taurus being an earthly Sign is the best Sign for planting many crops, such as potatoes, turnips, radishes and peanuts and all crops that grow quickly. In all our writing upon this subject we cannot help thinking that, as we are prepared in the knowledge of the Creator's law, and as we prepare and bring together the opportunity for this law to operate, it will do our work under the most adverse circumstances. If we do our part the All-Wise Ruler will do his. If we plant at the proper time, although the season promises but little, and see to it that all the opportunities are provided in a well enlivened soil, so that the electricity and moisture of the air and the dew of the night may be freely absorbed, we are assured, and by abundant tests have proven, that very much can be confidently expected under the most adverse circumstances. We know this to be true, for we have seen the most remarkable crops under the most adverse circumstances.

We are but the instruments, and but one of the many, which God in his infinite wisdom has provided to do his will, and he has so constituted us that our wants shall urge us on. Then let us see it in its proper light and be a cheerful agent and a zealous worker for his glory and our own prosperity." (p. 9-15.)

SECRETS OF BLACK ARTS!
I&M Ottenheimer, 1910s

"The old writers on Astrology and Magic give voluminous directions for gathering herbs and plants at certain periods during the waxing and waning of the Moon; but the more modern professors of the art, for the most part reject these formulas and rely rather upon the nature of the plants themselves, and upon the predominating stellar influences at the time their juices are expressed and prepared for use, for the efficacy of the various vegetable medicines used in Astrological Pharmacy. An English Astrologer who published a work on Chiromancy in 1671, insists in his preface thereto, that any plant bearing a resemblance to a portion of the human frame, is a specific for the diseases of the member which it is assimilated to. He gives several illustrations of his opinion, a few of which, modernized from the quaint and somewhat coarse language of the book, are cited below. How far facts will bear out the doctrine of affinities laid down by the author, the reader can ascertain by experiment.

Maiden Hair and the Moss of Quinces resemble the fibers of the head. Hence a decoction thereof is good for baldness.

Plants resembling the figure of the heart are comforting thereto. Therefore the Citron-apple, Fuller's Thistle, Spikenard, Balm, Mint, White-beet, parsley, and Motherwort, which bear in leaves and roots a heart-like form are congenial to that organ.

Herbs that simulate the shape of the lungs, as Sage, Lungwort, Hounds-tongue, and Comfrey, are good for pulmonary complaints.

Vegetable productions like in figure to the ears, as the leaves of Coltsfoot or wild Spikenard rightly prepared as a conserve and eaten, improve the hearing and memory. Oil extracted from the shells of sea-snails, which have the trimmings and curvature of the ears, also tends wonderfully to the cure of deafness.

When plants resemble the nose in their configuration, as the leaves of the Wild Water Mint; they are beneficial in restoring the sense of smell.

Certain plants having a semblance of the womb- as Birthwort or Heartwort, Ladies' Seal or Briony, etc., conduce much to a safe pregnancy. Shrubs and Herbs like unto the bladder and gall are excellent for those parts; as Night-shade, Alkakenge and Nux Visicaria. These relieve the gravel and stone.

Herbs formed like the milt, as Miltwort, Spleenwort, and Lupins, are recommended for the strengthening of that part of the human viscera.

Plants that are liver-shaped, as the herb Trinity, Liverwort, Agaric, fumitory and Figs, are efficacious in bilious diseases.

Walnuts, Indian Nuts, Leeks and the root of Ragwort, because of their form, are said when duly prepared to further generation and prevent sterility.

Herbs and Seeds, in shape like the teeth, as Toothwort, Pine Kernel, etc., preserve the dental organization. Plants of knobby form, like the knuckles or joints, as Galingale and the Snotty Odoriferous rush (Calamus,) are good for spinal complaints, renal diseases, foot gout, knee swellings, and ill joint pains whatsoever.

Oily vegetable products, as the Filbert, Walnut, Almond, etc., tend to fitness of body. Plants naturally lean emaciate those who take them; as Sarsaparilla, or long-leaved Rosa Solie.

Fleshy plants make flesh for the eaters; for instance the Onion, Leek and Colewort. Certain plants fortify and brace the nerves; for example, the Sensitive plant, Nettles, the roots of Mallorus, the herb Neuras, etc. The same are to be used as outward applications.

Herbs milky in their substance propagate milk; as

lettuce and the fruit of the Almond and Fig trees.

Plants of a serous nature purge the noxious humors between the flesh and the skin, as Spurge and Scamony.

Herbs whose acidity turns milk to curd, are said to lead to procreation. Such are Gallium, and the seeds of Spurge.

Those simples that obstruct the coagulation of milk, as Rue mixed with Cumin, will relieve a sore breast when the milk is knotted in it, if applied thereto.

Plants that are hollow, as the stalks of Grain, Reeds, Leeks, Garlic, etc., are good to purge, open and sooth the hollow parts of the body." (p. 43-46.)

TALISMANS

THE BLACK PULLET
18th Century

"Figure No. 1

Figure of the wand stained with the blood of the lamb.

These characters should be written on the wand with india ink.

'What do you wish to see at this moment, my son?' he asked me.

'The plain on which you found me at the point of death from pain and want,' I answered.

He raised his hands toward heaven and said, 'Soutram, Ubarsinens.' Immediately the spirits approached me and taking me in their arms, they lifted me, and I found myself transported to the foot of the pyramid. I saw a multitude of Arabs on horseback who were surveying it. Although I had not noticed him, the old man was near me enjoying my astonishment. 'You see, my son, how all the spirits are submissive to you, how they will obey you and await your orders. Do you wish to return to the place which you left or to soar for some time in the middle of the aerial parts? Do you know that you can see all that is happening around you and that you are visible only to the Great Being who wishes to accord you wisdom and to those who accompany you?' I testified to the desire to survey the immensity. 'Pronounce Saram while extending your arms towards the east, and you will be satisfied.' I uttered this word and made the indicated sign. The spirits lifted me up as well as the old man. We approached the clouds, and the vast horizon opened to my enchanted eyes.

The old man once again said to me: 'You see I have not made vain promises, you will have the same success in all your undertakings, but let us return to the pyramid. The spirits await us, and we will continue our workings.' He said 'Rabiam,' and very soon we re-entered the abode of the old man.

When we were seated, the spirits disappeared, only the first one remaining with us. All the insignia were changed, and a very intense light illuminated the vault. He then formed the second Magic Circle.

Figure 2

Placing himself therein, the old man said to me: 'Go near your spirit. I give you permission for I know that you have a pure heart, that you have never been guilty of any action which would make you blush. If that were not the case, you would be struck down dead on entering this circle. Go, my son.' I followed his instructions.

He opened the casket where all the rings were to be found, and drew out that one shown in Figure 3 as well as the talisman which he placed in my hands.

'This one will serve to conjure the celestial and infernal powers. Put the ring on your finger and the talisman over your heart, then pronounce the following words: Siras, Etar, Besanar, and you will perceive the effects.'

Figure 3

These characters should be engraved on the inside of the ring.

Hardly had these words come from my mouth than I saw a multitude of spirits and figures of different shapes. The spirit who was at my side said to me: 'Command and order and your desires will be satisfied.' The old man added, 'My son, the sky and the hells are at your orders. I think that at this moment you are not in want of anything; therefore, if you believe me, put off until later proving the intelligence and activity of these spirits. To make them disappear, remove the ring from your finger and the talisman from the place which it occupies, and they will return to their sphere.'

I did that which he ordered me to do, and they all went like a dream.

'There remain many things for me to teach you to make you at ease with these rings and talismans. This instruction will be the object of very important work which we shall do together with the help of our spirit. Let us follow the course of our experiences. Stay where you are.' He gave me another ring and talisman (Figure No. 4).

'These two precious objects, my son, are destined to make you loved by the most beautiful portion of the human race. There is not a woman who would not be happy to please you and who would not employ all possible means to be successful at it. Do you wish the most beautiful odalisque of the Grand Caliph should be brought before you in an instant? Put the ring on the second finger of your left hand, press the talisman against your lips, and say tenderly in a whisper: o Nades, Suradis, Manier.' Suddenly a spirit with rose-colored wings appeared; he placed himself on his knees before me. 'He awaits your orders,' the old man said. 'Say to him: Sader, Prostas, Solaster.' I repeated these words, and the spirit vanished. 'He is going to traverse an immense space with the rapidity of thought, and the most beautiful forms will appear before your eyes and will serve as a model to paint those houris which our Divine Prophet promises to his faithful servants. O my son, how blessed you are; not every mortal obtains from the Great Spirit such favors as I can see by the speed with which your wishes are executed.'

Figure 4

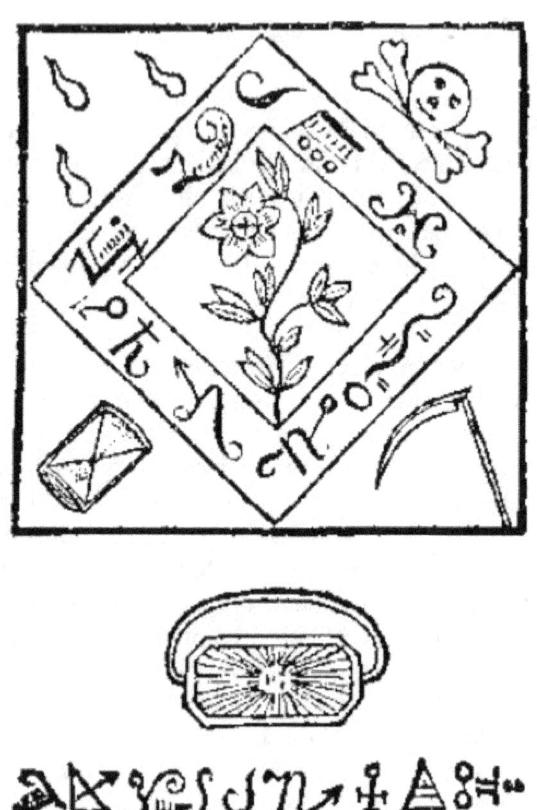

These characters should be engraved on the inside of the ring.

He had finished speaking when the spirit with the rose-colored wings arrived carrying in his arms a woman enveloped in a large white veil. She seemed to be asleep, and he placed her gently on a couch which appeared near me. He raised the veil which hid her. Never had anything so beautiful been offered to my eyes; she was Venus with all the charms of innocence. She sighed and opened the most beautiful eyes in the world which came to rest on me In a most harmonious voice she uttered a cry of surprise saying, 'It is he.' The old man told me to approach the beauty, place a knee on the ground, for it is thus that one should speak to her, and to take her hand. I obeyed, and the divinity to whom I addressed my homage said to me: 'I have seen thee in a dream, and the reality thereof makes thee more dear to my heart. I prefer you to the Sultan who for a long time has fatigued me with his homage.'

'That is enough,' said the old man, and he said forcefully, 'Mammes Laher.' Four slaves appeared to remove the couch and she who had made such a vivid impression on my heart. The old man noticed my emotion and the pain which resulted from her departure. He said to me, 'You will see her again. Understand that in order to possess wisdom, it is necessary to know how to resist the allurements of voluptuousness.'

His words made me come to myself, and I said to him, 'Pardon, my father, but you have seen her, that is my excuse.'

I replaced the ring and the talisman in the casket, and he gave me that which is illustrated in Figure No. 5.

Figure 5

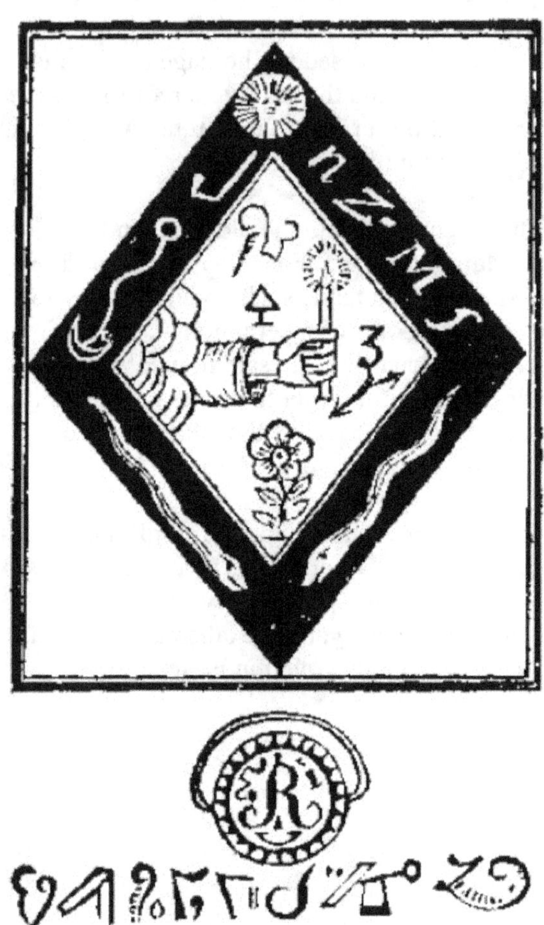

These characters should be engraved on the inside of the ring.

'This talisman and this ring are not less valuable. They will enable you to discover all the treasures which exist and to ensure you the possession of them. Place the ring on the second finger of your right hand, enclose the talisman with the thumb and little finger of your left hand, and say, Onaim, Perantes,

Rasonastos.' I repeated these three words, and seven spirits of a bronze color appeared, each carrying a large hide bag which they emptied at my feet. They contained gold coins which rolled in the middle of the hail where we were. I had not noticed that one of the spirits had on his shoulder a black bird, its head covered with a kind of hood. 'It is this bird,' the old man said to me, 'who has made them find all this treasure. Do not think that these are some of what you have seen here. You can assure yourself of this.' I replied, 'You are for me the truth itself. My father! Do you believe that I would insult you by doubting?' He made a sign, and the spirits replaced the gold in the bags and disappeared.

'You see, my son, what the virtues of these talismans and rings are. When you know them all, you will be able, without my aid, to perform such miracles as you judge proper. Replace in the casket those of which you have made proof, and take this one (Figure No. 6). They will enable you to discover the most hidden secrets; you will be able to penetrate everywhere without being seen, and not a single word in the universe can be uttered without it coming to your ears, whether you wish to listen to it yourself or to have it brought back to us by your agents when you order them to do so.'

Figure 6

These characters should be engraved on the inside of the ring.

'To prove it to you, repeat these words and place the talisman near your ear while you hold the ring tightly in your left hand: Nitrae, Radou, Sunandam.' I distinctly heard a voice which said to me: 'The Grand Mogul has decided in his private council that he must declare war on the Emperor of China.' Another voice said to me: 'All is rumor in Constantinople. Last night the Sultana was carried off, and the Grand Sultan is in despair. He has had all the eunuchs thrown into the sea after having had them beheaded.' 'Oh Heavens! What mischief I have done without wishing it,' I cried in pain. 'Well, my son,' the old man said, 'it is a lesson for you to learn- not to be enslaved by your passions and to know how to curb them. This is enough for today, tomorrow we will continue.'

The next day we followed the course of our mysterious operations. The spirit had not left us. 'You see, my son,' said the old man, 'that everything becomes easy with confidence and a pure soul without stain.' He opened the casket and took from it the talisman and ring (Figure No. 7).

When he had placed them in my hands, he pronounced two words, which I will teach you. 'Place this ring on the little finger of your left hand and the talisman to your right ear, and the most discreet man will divulge to you his most hidden thoughts. Here are the two words: Noctar, Raiban, and if you add a third word, which is Biranther, your greatest enemies will not be able to prevent themselves from loudly publishing their projects against you. In order to convince you, I am going to have appear before you one of the Beys of Cairo, and he will impart to you all of his schemes against the French.' He then said 'Nocdar,' to the spirit who then vanished like lightening. A quarter of an hour after he returned with the Bey who said: 'We have made a treaty of alliance with the English, and the armistice concluded with the French will be broken without warning.' He disappeared with the spirit after the old man had said: 'Zelander. The Mufti of the Grand Mosque will appear before your eyes and show you a manuscript of a work which he has composed and which he has refused to show to his best friends, even the Grand Visir.'

Figure 7

These characters should be engraved on the inside of the ring.

I did that which has previously been indicated, and very soon the Mufti appeared and placing his manuscript on the table, he said to me: 'Tonas, Zugar,' which means in the language of the magi: read and believe. The old man looked at him affectionately; he gave him his hand pronounced with sweetness and expression, 'O Solem.' The Mufti, after bowing, disappeared.

'Return the talisman and the ring to me,' the old man said, 'and take this.' (Figure No. 8)

'It will serve to activate as many spirits as you wish to undertake or to stop operations which would be contrary to you. The magic words are: Zorami, Zaitux, Elastot. We will not at this moment make any experiments; tomorrow we will go to the shores of the Nile and we will have constructed a bridge of a single arch on which we shall pass to the other side of the river. Here is the next talisman and its ring (Figure No. 9). They have the property of destroying everything, of commanding the elements, of calling down the thunder, hail, the stars, earthquakes, hurricanes, water spouts on land and sea, and of preserving our friends from all accidents. Here are the words which one must pronounce (the numbers indicate each thing that you wish to operate): first, you pronounce: Ditau, Hurandos; second, Ridas, Talimol; third, Atrosis, Narpida; fourth, Uusur, Itar; fifth, Hispen, Tromador; sixth, Paranthes, Histanos.'

Figure 8

These characters should be engraved on the inside of the ring.

'The talisman and the ring (Figure No. 10) will make you invisible to all eyes, even those of the spirits. Only the Great Being could be witness to your steps and your actions. You will penetrate everywhere into the bosom of the seas, into the bowels of the earth, you can likewise survey the airs, and no action of men can be hidden from you. Say only: Benatir, Cararkau, Dedos, Etinarmi.'

I repeated these four words, and through the walls of the

pyramid I saw two Arabs who were on the plain and who were profiting by the obscurity to ransack a tomb where they hoped to find something of value. 'You will be able, when you wish, to prove the other things which I will have taught you, it will only be necessary to place the ring successively on the different fingers of the right hand.'

'The talisman and ring (Figure No. 11) will serve to transport you into whatever part of the world you judge appropriate without running any danger. Say merely these words: Raditus, Polastrien, Terpandu, Ostrata, Pericatur, Ermas. But I hope that you will not make use of these means to leave me without my consent. Promise it to me.' 'My father, I swear to it.'

'With the talisman and the ring (Figure No. 12) you will be able to open all locks, no matter what secrets have been employed to shut them; you will not need a key. Simply by touching them with the ring and pronouncing these three words: Saritap, Pernisox, Ottarim, they will open of themselves without difficulty. Make proof of this on the spot, my son,' the old man told me. 'Close the casket which you see on that table.' I did this, and after having assured myself that nothing could open it but the key, I touched it with the ring and pronounced the magic words, and it opened of its own accord. 'It will be the same,' added the old man, 'with all the doors of prisons, fortified castles, where they might lock you up.'

'With the talisman and ring (Figure No. 13), you will be able to see what takes place in all houses without being obliged to enter them; you will be able to read the thoughts of everyone whom you approach and with whom you find yourself, and you will be able to render them service or do them injury as you wish. It will be sufficient to place the talisman on your head and then to blow on the ring saying: O Tarot, Nizael, Estarnas, Tantarez these words are for knowing the thoughts of people.

Figure 9

These characters should be engraved on the inside of the ring.

Figure 10

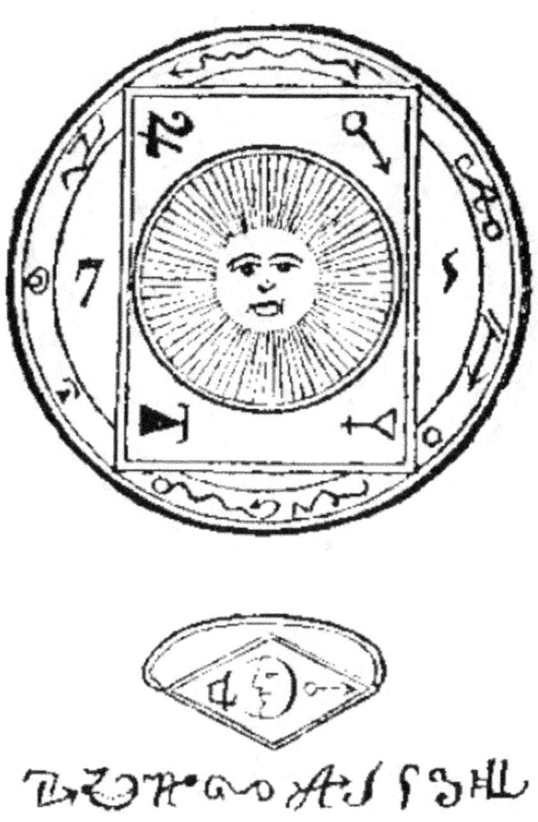

These characters should be engraved on the inside of the ring.

Figure 11

These characters should be engraved on the inside of the ring.

Figure 12

These characters should be engraved on the inside of the ring.

'In order to render service to those who deserve it, you say: Nista, Saper, Visnos, and they will immediately enjoy all sorts of prosperity. To punish the wicked and your enemies, you will say: Xatros, Nifer, Roxas, Rortos, and they will at once suffer punishment and frightful torment. What you have already seen should prove to you that I have advanced nothing which cannot be realized; therefore it is useless to make proof thereof.'

'The talisman and the ring (Figure No. 14) will serve you to destroy all the projects which could be made against you, and if any spirit wished to oppose your wishes, you could force him to submit to you. Place the talisman on a table under your left hand and with the ring on the second finger of the right hand, you say in a bass voice, while inclining your head: Senapos, Terfita, Estamos, Perfiter, Notarin. The talisman and ring (Figure No. 15) have a property as extraordinary as agreeable; they will give you all the virtues, all the talents, and the inclination to do good by changing all substances which are of a bad quality and rendering them excellent. For the first object, while elevating the talisman and with the ring placed on the first joint of the third finger of the left hand, it is sufficient to pronounce these words: Turan, Estonos, Fuza. For the second operation you say: Vazotas, Testanar, and you will see operate the wonder which I have proclaimed to you. The talisman and the ring (Figure No. 16) will assist you to know all the minerals and vegetables, their virtues and properties, and you will possess the universal medicine. There is no illness that you will not be able to cure and no cure that you will undertake without success. Aesculapius and Hippocrates will only be novices compared to you. You pronounce only these words: Reterrem, Salibat, Cratares, Hisater, and when you are near a sick person you will carry that talisman on the stomach and the ring with a St. Andrew's Cross around your neck on a ribbon the color of fire.

Figure 13

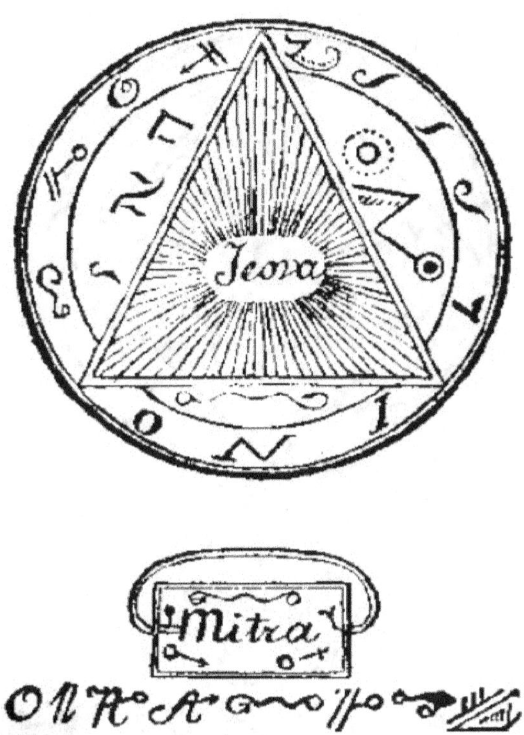

These characters should be engraved on the inside of the ring.

Figure 14

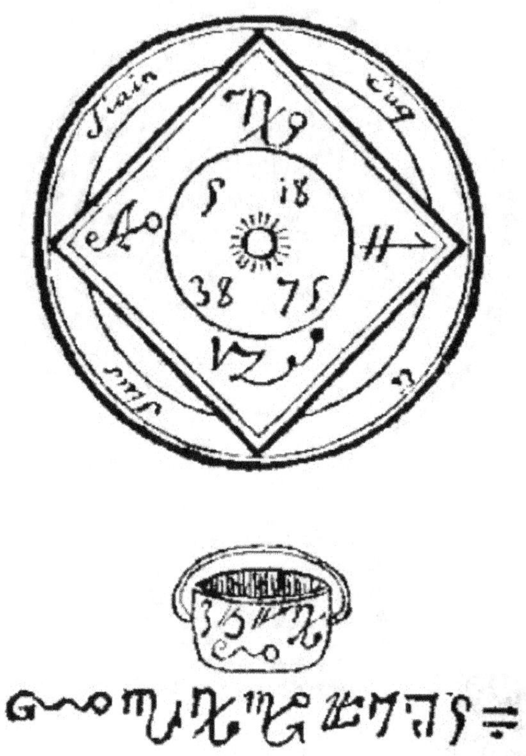

These characters should be engraved on the inside of the ring.

Figure 15

These characters should be engraved on the inside of the ring.

Figure 16

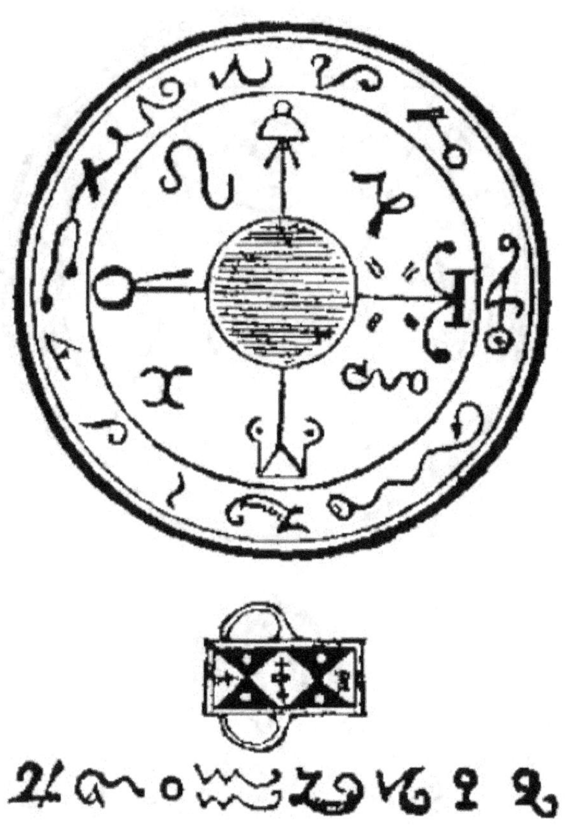

These characters should be engraved on the inside of the ring.

'The talisman and the ring (Figure No. 17) will keep you safe in the midst of the most ferocious animals, to subdue them to your will, to know by their different cries what they want as they have a language among themselves. Mad animals will keep at a distance from you, and you will make them perish forthwith by pronouncing the words which I am going to indicate to you.'

'For the first operation it is sufficient to say: Hocatos,

Imorad, Surater, Markila. For the second: Trumantrem, Ricona, Estupit, Oxa. The talisman and ring (Figure No. 18) will enable you to know the good or bad intentions of all the individuals whom you will meet to guarantee you of it and to impress on their face a mark which will be noticed by everyone. It is sufficient to pronounce these mysterious words, while placing the talisman on your heart and the ring on the little finger of your right hand. You will then say: Crostes, Furinot, Katipa, Garinos. The talisman and the ring (Figure No. 19) will give you all talents and a profound understanding of all the arts so that you can perform with as much brilliance as the greatest masters and foremost artists. It is sufficient to carry the talisman and the ring in a manner you judge suitable while pronouncing these seven words: Ritas, Onalun, Tersorit, Ombas, Serpitas, Quitathar, Zamarath while adding afterwards the name of the art or the talent which you wish to possess. The talisman and the ring (Figure No. 20) will help you to win at lotteries and to make certain when playing a game that you will obtain the fortune of your adversaries. You will place the talisman on your left arm, adjusting it with a white ribbon, and the ring on the little finger of your right hand; then you will say these words: Rokes for a selection, Pilatus for a combination of two numbers, Zotas for dice, Tulitas for four winning numbers, Xatanitos for five winning numbers. Be sure to pronounce all the words when you are on a quine, and for a card game you will pronounce them each time the cards are shuffled, if it is you or your partner, and before commencing you will touch your left arm on the spot where the talisman is to be found with your right hand, and you will kiss your ring. All this must be done without drawing the attention of your adversary.'

Figure 17

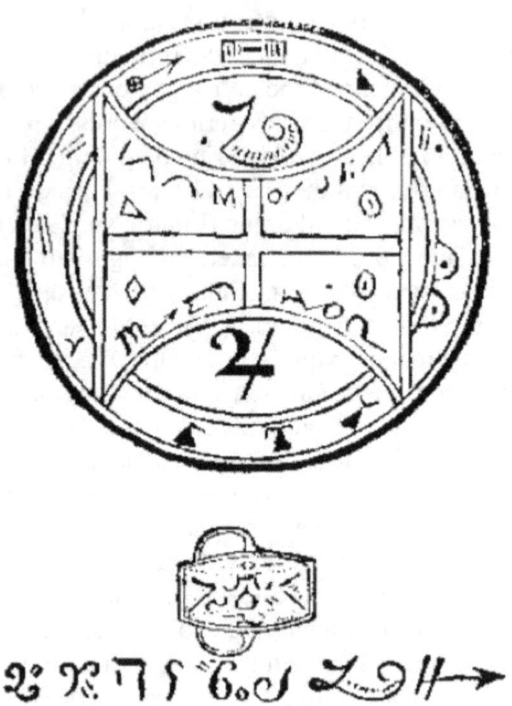

These characters should be engraved on the inside of the ring.

Figure 18

These characters should be engraved on the inside of the ring.

Figure 19

These characters should be engraved on the inside of the ring.

Figure 20

These characters should be engraved on the inside of the ring.

'The talisman and the ring (Figure No. 21) will enable you to direct all the infernal powers against your enemies or against those who would injure your friends. You will carry it in a manner which you consider suitable and pronounce merely these three words: Osthariman, Visantiparos, Noctatur. The talisman and the ring (Figure No. 22) will serve you to recognize what the infernal powers wish to undertake, and you can abort all their projects by placing the talisman on your chest and the ring on the first joint of the little finger of the left hand.

You pronounce these words: Actatos, Catipta, Bejouran, Itapan, Marnutus. As it is possible that you have not had the means of making talismans and rings similar to mine,' the old man said to me, 'you will make them up in the manner which I will indicate. Know that the rings are of bronzed steel with the characters engraved thereon. The talismans should be made of silk cloth in the dimensions of the figures.'

Figure 21

These characters should be engraved on the inside of the ring.

Figure 22

These characters should be engraved on the inside of the ring.

No. 1. White satin embroidered in gold.

No. 2. Red satin embroidered in silver.

No. 3. Sky-blue satin embroidered in silver.

No. 4. Black satin embroidered in silver.

No. 5. Green satin embroidered in gold.

No. 6. Violet satin embroidered in silver.

No. 7. Golden-yellow satin embroidered in gold.

No. 8. Lilac satin with shaded silk.

No. 9. Poppy-red satin embroidered in silver.

No. 10. Yellow satin embroidered in black silk.

No. 11. Puce satin embroidered in gold.

No. 12. Dark blue satin embroidered in silver.

No. 13. Pale gray satin embroidered in gold.

No. 14. Rose satin embroidered in silver.

No. 15. Golden-yellow satin embroidered in silver.

No. 16. Orange satin embroidered in silver.

No. 17. Dark green satin embroidered in gold.

No. 18. Black satin embroidered in gold.

No. 19. White satin embroidered in black silk.

No. 20. Cherry satin embroidered in silver.

No. 21. Grey-White satin, shaded.

No. 22. Red satin, embroidered in the middle with gold, the border in silver, and the signs in black and white silk.

The old man, after having given me this information, replaced all the talismans and rings in the casket. The spirit who was at my side closed it and gave him the key. The old man said to me: 'All the wonders which have been performed in front of You, my dear son, ought not to leave any doubt of the power and virtue of these talismans and rings. If you have not experienced any obstacle in your enterprises, it is because your heart is pure, that your soul is without stain, and that virtue, probity, and honor will always be dear to you. A man who had the least reproach to make to himself, who had destroyed the good of others, or who had only the intention of so doing, would not be able to participate in our mysteries. In vain would he have in his possession all that you see, our magical language known to him. The celestial powers- aerial, infernal, terrestrial, and those of the oceans and fire- would rebel against him. All that he wished to undertake would turn to his shame and his confusion, and at each invocation which he might make, the powers that he implored for help and intervention would answer him: Renounce thy projects. Thou art guilty. Before commanding us, purify thyself, expiate thy faults. If after these emanations he continued to conjure the powers, he would finish by being punished and would without fail lose his life. Remember then, my dear son, that all is possible with virtue and that not one fault will remain unpunished. There are still two prayers which you must be careful to recite before and after each conjuration that you wish to do; here they are:

FIRST PRAYER

The Celestial Fire above is an incorruptible flame, always scintillating, the source of life, fountain of all the beings, and principle of all things. This flame produces all and nothing perishes except which it consumes: it makes itself known by itself. This fire cannot be contained in any place; it is without body or matter. It encompasses the skies, and from it emanates a little spark which makes all fire of the Sun, of the Moon, and the Stars. That is what I know of God: do not try to know more because that is beyond you, such judge as thou art. Moreover, know that the unjust or wicked man can-not hide himself in front of God; no address or any excuse can disguise anything from his piercing eyes. All is clear to God: God is everywhere.

SECOND PRAYER

There is in God as immense profundity of flame; the heart ought not, however, to fear to touch or to be touched by this adorable fire; it will not be consumed by this sweet fire, whose tranquil and perishable heat makes the union, harmony, and duration of the world. Nothing exists except by this fire which is God. No one has engendered it; it is without mother, it knows all, and no one is able to know anything of it. It is immovable in its projects and its name is ineffable. Here then is that which is God; because for us, who are his messengers, we are but a small part of God." (p. 32-66.)

THE PETIT ALBERT
18th Century

"Ancient Talismans and the Usage Thereof

The great reputation Paracelsus has gained in the world by the deep science of his works gives much authority to this writing. It provides, as an indubitable thing, that if we form talismans according to the method he gives, they will produce effects that will surprise those who will experience them. This is what I experienced myself with admiration; a very happy and successful life. Here in what way he speaks in his magical archidoxis.

Nobody can, without temerity, cast doubt that the stars and celestial planets have the most dominant influences on everything that is in this lower world; for since we see and that we essentially feel that domination the planets, their influences on man, who is the image of God and has the advantage of reason; how much more so should we believe that they dominate and affect metals, stones, and whatever nature and art can produce; since all these things are lower than man, and more capable of receiving, without resistance, their influences since they are deprived of reason and free will, and that man has the advantage that he is able to use these material things, for it to attract the influences of the stars?

But what is worthy of being known and well noticed is that the seven planets in the cosmos never influence more effectively than through the seven metals of their own nature, that is to say, which have sympathy with their substance. About this the wise Kabbalists that experienced by the sublime penetration of their sciences, what are the specific metals to planets, they determined gold for the Sun, the day of Sunday, argentum to the Moon, to Monday, iron to Mars, to Tuesday, the quicksilver for Mercury, to Wednesday, tin to Jupiter, to

Thursday, copper to Venus, to Friday, and lead to Saturn, the Saturday. On this basis, we give here the way of making talismans, which the ancient sages referred to as the seals of the planets.

Talisman Of the Sun For Sunday

```
 6 32 13  3 33 23
 7 31 27 28 28 30
19 14 16 15 23 24
18 20 22 21 17 13
32 22 10 19 26 12
36 15 15 14 18 13
```

This talisman must be composed with the most exquisite and purest of gold, which is that of Arabia or of Hungary. Here it is formed into a round plate, well polished on both sides; and upon one of these sides we draw a square composed of six lines of numbers that thus progress from one corner to another, shaped into the semblance of St. Andrew's cross. There are one hundred and eleven. And that is mysterious as well, and all be informed is that the numbers which will be marked in all talismans or seals of the planets are large numbers of stars that are under the control of each planet, and they lord over their attributes as their subjects, and this is why those who are versed in astrology, called precursors planets or stars premieres, and they are confluent and present, they have others under their direction, for the distribution of their influences. On the other side of the plate, you have to brand the hieroglyphic figure of the planet, which is crowned king in his royal throne, holding in his right hand a scepter on the head with the Sun, with the sun on his head and the name of 'Soliel', and brandishing his scepter with a roaring lion at his feet. And so that this operation is done accurately and in suitable circumstances, you will etch with two very clean irons everything I said above, not to lose the favorable moment of the constellation, because it is necessary that printing is done at the time that the sun will be in conjunction with the moon in the first degree of Leo; And when the gold plate will be marked on both sides with the above irons, you must promptly wrap the same in a thin cloth. The two engraved irons, must likewise be utilized in making the talismans of other planets; printing must be done in the favorable moment of the constellation, because you must know that it is in this moment that the planet spreads and likewise prints its benign influences on the talisman, is a supernatural way and the whole mystery. The properties of this talisman of the sun are that the person who will wear it with confidence and reverence, will become pleasant to the powers of the earth, kings, princes, the nobles, which will then exhibit kindness and mercy.

Talisman Of the Moon For Monday

```
37 78 29 70 21 62 13 45  5
 6 38 79 30 71 22 63 14 46
47  7 59 80 31 72 23 55 15
16 48  8 40 81 32 64 24 56
57 17 49  9 41 73 33 65 25
26 58 18 50  1 42 74 34 66
67 27 59 19 51  2 43 75 35
35 68 19 60 11 52  3 44 76
77 28 69 20 61 12 53  4 45
```

This talisman must be composed with the most pure silver that can be found, which should be made into a round plate, well polished; On the front side, engrave nine lines of numbers, each of which will contain the mysterious number of three hundred sixty nine, as shown in the swuare above. On the other side of the plate, must be printed the hieroglyphic image of the planet- a woman covered with a large and wide dress with both feet on the ground, branches in her right hand, and a star of great brilliance upon her head with the word, 'Luna'. The operation must be performed on a Monday of spring, when we will have the first degree of Capricorn or Virgo in favorable aspect to Jupiter or Venus. Wrap the talisman in a white cloth; and it will be greatly useful to destroy diseases; it will preserve travelers from harm and ward off thieves; it will cause laborers to be favorable to merchants.

Talisman Of Mars For Tuesday

    This talisman must be formed on a polished and round plate, of the best iron. The mysterious numbers will be sixty five. And on the other side of the plate will be formed the hieroglyphic figure of the face of the planet, representing a soldier, holding in his left hand a shield, and the right a sword, having a star on his head, with the name of Mars.

<pre>
14 10 5 12 18
20 12 6 32 24
21 27 14 9 15
22 13 19 15 26
23 1 20 16 18
</pre>

The printing instruments must be made of finely tempered steel, and the printing is done in the time we have observed that the Moon is in a benign and favorable appearance with some other planet, between the first degree of the sign of Aries or Sagittarius; and it is good, if as talisman plate is put at the burning furnace, to blast the plate in a furnace before printing to make it more suitable for receiving the etching of mysterious figures. When it is cooled, wrap it in a piece of red taffeta. This talisman will have the property of rendering invulnerable those that perform the will of the cosmos reverently, and to give him power and an extraordinary force; he will win his battles. The planet Mars affects so marvelously on this talisman, when it is done accurately, that if it is buried in the foundations of a fortress, it becomes impregnable, and those who want to undertake the attack, are destroyed. And if it is formed when the constellation of Mars is in opposition to the retrograde planets favorably, it will bring bad luck wherever it is put, and there cause dissensions, rebellions, and civil war; I know that a great statesman wore a similar talisman in England, in the time of the revolution of Cromwell.

Talisman Of Mercury For Wednesday

This talisman must be formed on a round plate of fixed mercury, (I will give below the way to fix mercury for talismans, as I have done this myself.) When the plate is made and polished it is printed with the irons on one side, with the mysterious number of two hundred and sixty, distributed in eight lines, as seen here represented.

And on the other side of the plate is the hieroglyphic figure of the planet Mercury, representing an angel with wings on her back and its heels, holding in its right hand a caduceus shaped scepter, and a star on its head, with the name of Mercury. Print the talisman in a favorable time of the constellation, as will be observed before starting the business. And when it is completed, wrap the talisman in a cloth of purple colored silk.

```
 8  8 59 43  4 64 63 11
49 16 14 52 52 14 10 56
41 43 22 24 34 29 18 49
32 34 35 29 29 38 39 24
40 32 27 37 30 30 31 33
17 47 46 21 20 43 42 24
 9 55 54 12 13 51 50 16
64 12  3 12 50  6 77 57
```

This talisman will have the property of making the bearer eloquent and give them great stealth, and and will aid them in studying the sciences. If the talisman is placed in your wine for only an hour, it makes the memory so happy that it may recall everything with ease; it can even cure all kinds of fevers. If you put it under the head of the bed, it provides prophetic, lucid dreams.

Talisman Of Jupiter For Thursday

```
16  3   2 13
15 15   1  3
 9  6   7 12
 4 14 14  2
```

This talisman must be formed on a round plate, made
from the purest tin. Print on one side of the mysterious number
of the planet, which is thirty four distributed in four lines, as we
see here. And on the other side of the plate is printed the
hieroglyphic figure of the face of the planet, to be a man dressed
in robes, holding in his hands a book, which he seems to read,
and above his head a shining star, with this word; Jupiter. Begin
printing the mysterious figures on the plate, with irons, when
you shall observe that the constellation of the planet will be
favorable, when the moon enters the first degree of Libra, with
Jupiter in good aspect with the sun. When the operation is

finished, you will wrap the talisman in a piece of blue silk. This talisman will give to those who will carry it reverently the love and support of those which they wish it from. The bearer will continually gain more wealth. It will make the bearer fortunate in trading, commerce, and in all enterprises; it dissipates sorrows, cares, and unwelcome challenges.

Talisman Of Venus For Friday

This talisman must be formed on a round copper plate well purified and polished. Print on one side of the mysterious number five hundred and seventy, distributed in seven lines, as marked here.

And on the other side of the plate is the hieroglyphic figure of the face of the planet, which is to be a woman lasciviously dressed, having close to his right thigh a cherubim holding a bow and a fiery arrow, and the woman holds in her left hand a musical instrument, like a guitar, and above its head a shining star, with this sword, Venus. Printing will be done with the irons, in the moment that the constellation of Venus will be in good aspect with some favorable planet, the Moon being in in the first degree of Taurus or Virgo. The operation being finished, the talisman must be wrapped in green silk. And he who will wear this talisman can ensure the good graces of those that he desires, and to be loved passionately, both by women and men. It also has the virtue of reconciling foes, causing them to cease fighting and drink together, such that they become friends; it also makes the wearer talented at playing all manner of music.

```
22 47 16 41 10 35  4
25 23 48 17 42 11  9
30  6 24 49 18 36 12
13 31  7 25 43 19 37
30 14 32  1 26 44 20
21 39  8 32  2 17 45
46 15 40  9 35  3 27
```

Talisman Of Saturn For Saturday

This talisman must be formed on a round plate, out of the purest lead, and you will print on the front side, this mysterious number, distributed in fifteen lines, following the layout shown here.

2 4 9
7 5 3
6 1 8

And on the other side of the plate, will be put the hieroglyphic figure of the face of the planet, which will be a bearded old man, holding in his hand a kind of pickaxe, hunched over somewhat, and above his head will be a star with the word, Saturn. You will start printing the mysterious figures with your irons when you have observed that Saturn is in a constellation of favorable aspect, the moon entering the first degree with the sign of Taurus or Capricorn. And when the operation is over, you must wrap the talisman in a black silk fabric piece.

This talisman is of great help, first, for women who are in search of childbirth because they are suffering almost no pain from the same; multiple individuals have tested this manner of the talisman. It also multiplies and increases the things with which it is placed- If a rider carries the talisman in his left boot, his horse will not be injured in any way. It has all the effects contrary to these, when it is formed in the time that the constellation of Saturn is in a disastrous situation and a retrograde moon is in the above signs.

Forming Plaques For the Talismans, In Mercury

Choose a Wednesday in Springtime, when Mercury's constellation is on either side with the sun and Venus, and after invoking the spirit of Mercury controlling this planet, prepare the necessary materials, in the following manner: sal ammoniac, verdegris, Roman vitriol, two ounces of each well pulverized. Put it all together in an iron pot, with three quarts of water, and heat it so that everything boils up reducing down to a pint of liquid, and then add two ounces of mercury, and stir it well with a spoon until they become thick and homogenized; then let them cool, and subsqeuently filter the liquid out. At the bottom, a bit of gray sediment will remain, which you must wash with water, two or three times, always filtering out the liquid each time, and then spread the paste on a flat, polished wooden plank, allowing the sun to dry the same. After this add two ounces of good earth, and much Senna powder, and put it all in a sealed crucible luted with another crucible attached, so that both when placed together end to end make a single vessel without an opening, and so that nothing can evaporate when the vessels are heated. These crucibles must be sealed together with a loam paste of horse dung and iron filings. Do not put the luted crucible in the furnace, but rather a simple stove, and make sure the vessels are completely dry before you begin this work. When the crucible has been cooking for one hour, increase the heat until the vessels begin to change color. At the third hour the fire will be increased again, and you must continuously feed the fire with bellows, then leave the crucible to cool. The material will have collected at the bottom of the lower vessel, in small grains, and you must take these grains, mix them with borax, and place them in a new vessel; this being done you will have a very fine fixed, granulated mercury, clean and pure for forming talismans or mysterious rings that have the property of attracting the benign influences of the planet Mercury, provided that your work is correct according to the rules of art.

Formulating Talismans Used by Other Kabbalists

You will use the same metal plates which were spoken of before. Start the operation at such hours and appropriate moments to attract the benign influences of the celestial forces spoken of for each; on one side of the plate is printed, squarely shaped, characters that are marked below; that is to say, for the Sun, those that are found in the first line. For the Moon, those that are found in the second line. For Mars, those we find in the third line. For Mercury, those, which can be found on the fourth line. For Jupiter, those we find in the fifth line. For Venus, those we found in the sixth line. For Saturn, those we find in the seventh line. You can engrave the other side of the plate with the same figures spoken of before, and you will experience wonderful effects. I have no doubt that, if that book falls from my hands into those of people of small minds, being ignorant, they will become superstitious; because they will imagine that the admirable wonders I treat of here are made by the ministry of evil spirits; for, they say, how can we understand that a metal plate, in charge of some characters and figure, operates things that surpass the ordinary forces of nature? I refute these kinds of people and say thus: So you believe that evil spirits can do those things which surpass the usual order of nature? But why, then, do not you think the creator of the universe is powerful enough to be imprinted upon all of nature itself? Why do you not instead acknowledge that he who gave our race the secret to attract to itself under a heavy mass of iron, such forces, from the celestial regions to the earthly, is powerful enough to give force to the stars, which are creatures infinitely more perfect than humans, and also those which are even more precious, upon the earth? These have properties and secrets of virtues, which surpass the reach of our minds, especially as these stars are governed by heavenly intelligences which regulate their movements.

But how difficult can it be to believe that from characters or certain numbers on a metal plate, can be produced many wonders, since it is believed that one can obviously see that in some small parts of spherical materials, triangular rows come from the same in a certain order, produce admirable effects, not only to attract a mass of iron, but always turn the needle compasses in the direction of the North Star, and adjust the dials to the sun, and such?

FOLK MAGIC, SUPERSTITION, AND CHARMS

I wish I was able to ask these unscrupulous people, why in Switzerland to even today, where there are many snakes, because of the mountains, why do these snakes fear the following in Greek, and if they hear the three words "osy, osya, osy" they quickly clog one of their ears with the tip of their tail and flatten themselves sideways against the ground, so as not to hear these words, such that they are unable to bring harm to people? If I am told that it is nature that produces this instinct in them, why would nature be less ingenious in other creatures?" (p. 39-55.)

BOOK OF FORBIDDEN KNOWLEDGE
Johnson &co. 1910s

"Talismans

In the whole circle of the occult sciences there is scarcely anything more abstruse or intricate than the mystical science of Talismans. The use of them has occasionally received much opposition from incredulous individuals; while on the other hand, it has stood the ground with firmness amidst the change of ages. Mourning rings, miniatures. lockets, mementos, armorial bearings, and the 'boast of heraldry,' are but so many relics of Talismanic learning, among mankind in general, there is much of talismanic belief; witness the avidity with which the caul of an infant is sought after to preserve from danger by water; as also the celebrated romance of *The Talisman*, by Sir Walter Scott; the intense interest of which arises from the narration of a singular instance of the faith formerly reposed in Talismanic agency. It is now well known that when Napoleon went to Egypt he was then presented with a talisman by a learned eastern magician, the effect of which was to protect and defend him from sudden attacks, assassinations, and all manner of hurts from firearms.

TALISMAN FOR LOVE

This Talisman is said to be wonderfully efficacious in procuring success in amours and love adventures. It should be made or prepared when Venus, the planet of love, is the evening star. It should be made preferably of pure silver, but where that is not practicable, cut out the picture of the Talisman from this book, and paste it neatly in any suitable article, such as in a locket, back of a watch, or it may be pasted on a piece of round cardboard of equal size and worn over the heart or the left breast. or carried in the pocket as a Lucky Pocket Piece.

TALISMAN AGAINST ENEMIES

Where possible this Talisman should be cast of the purest grain tin, and during the increase of the moon. The characters are to be engraved on it also during the increase of the moon. Where this is not practicable, the illustration may be cut out of this book and placed in, say, a locket, and suspended about the neck, or worn on any part of the body, or it may be pasted on a piece of round cardboard of equal size and carried in the pocket. It should be kept from the sight of all but the wearer. Its effects are to give victory over enemies, protection against their machinations, and to inspire the wearer thereof with the most remarkable confidence.

TALISMAN FOR WAR AND BATTLE

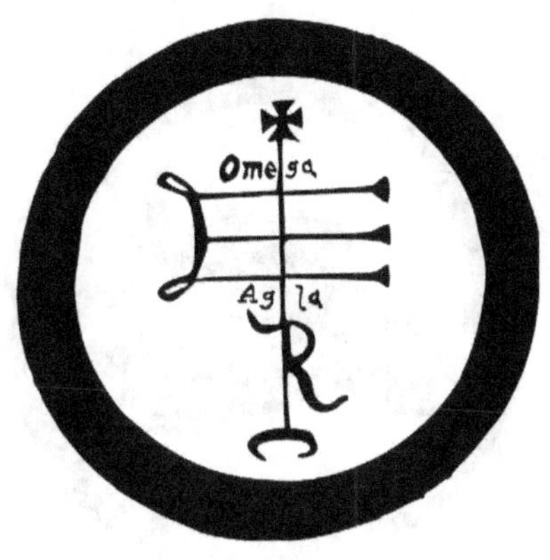

This Talisman bears on it the powerful words, and also the awful sign which were said to have been conveyed to the Emperor Constantine from heaven, in daylight, and in the presence of his whole army, and whereby he was victorious in battle. It should be made of highly tempered steel, but where not practicable, the illustration may be cut out of this book and placed in a locket or other suitable article, or simply pasted on a piece of cardboard of similar size. It should be tied around the sword arm. An ancient manuscript says of this Talisman: 'He that beareth this sign about him shall be helped in every need and necessity.'

TALISMAN FOR DESTROYING INSECTS AND REPTILES

This Talisman is to be made, if possible, of iron, when the sun and moon enter the sign, Scorpio. It has been proved to be powerful in effect; so much so that no kind of venomous reptile or troublesome insect can't come within some yards of the house or place in which it is. The manuscript from which the account of this Talisman is taken, cost a very large sum and a medical gentleman to whom it belonged, affirms that he had himself proved its efficacy, for being at one time much annoyed with beetles, he made a talisman, according to instructions here given and screwed it to the floor, when these troublesome insects immediately disappeared, but afterwards, when the servant removed it, through ignorance, they returned in great numbers; when he again nailed it to the floor, and they again disappeared!

If impractical to have this Talisman specially made, the illustration may be cut out of this book and pasted on a piece of heavy tin or other metal, or even a stout piece of cardboard." (p.48-52.)

THE POWER OF GEMS AND CHARMS
Geo Bratley, 1906

"Talismanic Engraved Jewels

In this branch of our subject we approach the true science of talismans, charms, and amulets, and trespass on the fringe of practical magic. But little can be given along practical lines in a work written for the general public, for this branch must always apply to the individual, and the efficacy of the talismanic gem will depend on the time of birth and the planetary positions on the day; so that only with a knowledge of astrology can the talisman be constructed with the correct metal, gem, and design, and the right time taken for the making of it. As it is impossible to give the special talisman to each reader, we will give those names and designs which may be used for the month of birth and engraved on the birthstone or metal so as to enhance its natural magical power.

Gems are not classed as talismanic till they have passed through the engravers hands, where they are engraved and set cabalistically; up till that time they are charms depending on their natural or artificial power. The Gnostics, Kabalists, and other occultists of the middle ages considered that this natural power of the gem was greatly enhanced by this process. The Egyptians, being great believers in astrology, were accustomed to have an engraving of one of the signs of the Zodiac on some gem which was mounted as a ring. The Romans favored engravings of certain gods and goddesses; Venus engraved on onyx was supposed to impart strength and beauty; Jupiter gave the necessary ambition to honors and renown; the beryl, engraved with a frog and set in gold in the form of a pendant, is a great love talisman; the cornelian, bearing a man with a scepter, the sardonyx, engraved with an eagle, are good for fortune; the topaz, with a falcon, procures sympathy for its possessor; the red coral, with a man bearing a sword, will protect the wearer from epidemics; the onyx, inscribed with the head of a camel, will produce frightful dreams.

Very potent for good or evil are some of the geometrical designs, such as Solomon's seal, the pentacle and pentacle, the seals of the planets, their magic squares, the signs and names of the planetary spirits, and many other curious figures which are used to bring the wearer into touch with the denizens of other planes. The appropriate metal in which to have set the birth-gem and the design or name to have engraved on the metal or gem will be found in the following table.

GEM	METAL	NAME	DESIGN
Garnet	Lead	Tzakmaqiel	Water Bearer
Amethyst	Tin	Vacabiel	The Fishes
Bloodstone	Iron	Sarahiel	The Ram
Sapphire	Copper	Araziel	The Bull
Emerald	Platinum	Saraiel	The Twins
Agate	Silver	Phakiel	The Crab
Ruby	Gold	Seratiel	The Lion
Sardonyx	Platinum	Schaltiel	The Virgin
Chrysolite	Copper	Chadakiel	The Scales
Opal	Iron	Sartziel	The Scorpion
Topaz	Tin	Saritiel	The Horse
Turquoise	Lead	Semaqiel	The Goat

The name or design may be engraved alone or both if desired. The designs may be found in any almanac, and can easily be copied from Zadkiels. Each of these engraved jewels has special rule over various affairs connected with life besides bringing good luck to those who wear them by right of birth. More than one may be worn at the same time, but it must be remembered, as previously stated, that in all cases the birthstone must always be worn. The affairs and events they have rule over, and the class of people they should be worn by are given below. The numbers corresponding to those in first column of the foregoing table.

1. For good health, content, and to develop the psychic powers. Should be worn by the sick and depressed or those desirous of seeking into the mysteries of nature.

2. For protection from evil influences and enemies, gives dominion over the passions and animal nature. Those who wish to break the fetters of vice, or cement broken friendships, should possess this jewel.

3. For fruitfulness and propagation. Should be worn by the newly married; by those interested in husbandry and the breeding of animals.

4. For financial matters, and prospers all transactions and enterprises. Of value to speculators, bankers, and those dealing with money.

5. For success in travel and changes ; protects against dangers and mishaps in travel on land or water. Should be worn by sailors, commercial travelers, and all those having much activity.

6. Gives luck in connection with legacies and wills; is helpful for the discovery of hidden treasure; confers eloquence and enlightens the mind. Orators, actors, and those interested in mining and seeking of treasure should have this jewel.

7. Good for pleasure, hazardous risks, harmonious relations with children, success to actors, and in all love matters. Should be worn by gamblers; those connected with the stage; is of luck to children, to teachers, and those who seek to gain the affections of the opposite sex.

8. For health; success to servants; gives luck in the breeding of small animals and poultry. Should be used by the sick; those in subordinate positions; breeders of dogs, cats, birds, etc.

9. For friendship, justice, marriage, or law. Useful to those who are engaged to marry, or who are married; to judges, lawyers, and all those seeking favor or friendship.

10. Success in warfare, contests, dangerous pursuits, and in handling medicine. Soldiers, doctors, chemists, surgeons, those entering into contests, or wherever there is risk to life should wear this.

11. Gives success to voyagers, emigrants, pioneers, and those living in foreign countries. Should be used by adventurers, explorers, those going abroad or dealing with foreigners.

12. For honor, preferment, seeking favor, for enlightening the understanding and conferring reason. To be worn by those seeking position or the favor of those in authority. Politicians and rulers should possess this jewel.

It may be that there are those who would like to follow in the steps of Apollonius and change their gems daily. If so the gems given to each day may be converted into potent talismans and worn on their day irrespective of birth data. They will be as below:

Sunday: A ruby or chrysolite set in gold, and engraved on the gem or metal a scepter king upon a lion, or a queen with a scepter.

Monday: A selenite, pearl, or opal set in silver; the design, a king riding on a doe, or a woman with a bow and arrow.

Tuesday: An amethyst or bloodstone set in iron; design, a king on a wolf, or a female warrior.

Wednesday: An olivine, agate, or jade set in platinum; design, a king riding upon a bear, or a woman spinning.

Thursday: An emerald or sapphire set in tin; design, a king with a javelin riding on a stag, or a woman bedecked with flowers.

Friday: A turquoise, beryl, or lapis lazuli set in copper; design, a king on a camel, or a naked maiden.

Saturday: An onyx set in lead; design, a king, crowned and seated on a dragon, or a witch." (p. 76-80) *The Power of Gems and Charms*, Geo Bratley, 1906.

GEMS AND STONES

ARADIA, THE GOSPEL OF THE WITCHES
Edward Waite, 1899

"The Spell or Conjuration of the Round Stone:

The finding of a round stone, be it great or small, is a good sign, but it should never be given away, because the receiver will then get the good luck, and some disaster befall the giver. On finding a round stone, raise the eyes to heaven, and throw the stone up three times (catching it every time), and say:

Spirit of good omen,
Who art come to aid me,
Believe I had great need of thee.
Spirit of the Red Goblin,
Since thou hast come to aid me in my need,
I pray of thee do not abandon me;
I beg of thee to enter now this stone,
That in my pocket I may carry thee,

And so when anything is needed by me,
I can call unto thee: be what it may,
Do not abandon me by night or day.
Should I lend money unto any man
Who will not pay when due, I pray of thee,
Thou the Red Goblin, make him pay his debt!
And if he will not and is obstinate,
Go at him with thy cry of "Brie- brie!"

And if he sleeps, awake him with a twitch,
And pull the covering off and frighten him!
And follow him about where'er he goes.
So teach him with thy ceaseless "Brie- brie!"
That he who obligation e'er forgets

Shall be in trouble till he pays his debts.
And so my debtor on the following day
Shall either bring the money which he owes,

Or send it promptly: so I pray of thee,
O my Red Goblin, come unto my aid!
Or should I quarrel with her whom I love,
Then, spirit of good luck, I pray thee go
To her while sleeping - pull her by the hair,
And bear her through the night unto my bed!
And in the morning, when all spirits go
To their repose, do thou, ere thou return'st

Into thy stone, carry her home again,
And leave her there asleep. Therefore, O Sprite!
I beg thee in this pebble make thy home!
Obey in every way all I command.
So in my pocket thou shalt ever be,
And thou and I will ne'er part company"

(p. 27-28.)

LIBER SALOMONIS
16th Century

"And Solomon said know that in the first *ala* or wing be twenty four precious stones great and of great power to similitude, and they signify that there be twenty four hours in the day and night. Solomon began and said: I put the first stone of ruby, for that it is brighter and clearer and fairer and of more price above all other stones. And I will speak now of its color and its power and its virtue, and of his seal and of his figure that ought to be in it. And thus I shall say in all other stones. Each stone signifies stability without end. The color of Ruby is as the color of fire. And its power is that it shines by night as a star or as a flame. And the virtue of it is that it makes good color of men that bear it reverently. And it increases his good of this world among other men. And the image which you ought to put in the same ought to be as Draco, that is a dragon, of terrifying power.

The second stone is Topaz of which the color is yellow as of gold. Its power is that if it be put in a cauldron with boiling water it will prevent it from boiling.. And the virtue of it is that it makes a man chaste that bears it with him and it gives favor from great Lords. And its figure is a Falcon.

The third stone is emerald. This stone is green and fair, and it is not as heavy as many others. And its power is to keep the light, and it heals the face. And it does many wonderful things. And its virtue is to increase riches. And who that bears it in gold is able to predict the future. And the figure of it is a scarab.

The fourth stone is jacinth the color of which is red and gray as the grayness of an apple. Of these there will be some which are more red and some more gray. Its power is that he that bears it is not infected with sickness. Its virtue is that it gives health and honor, and keeps the man bearing it safe in his travels. And its figure is a lion well figured.

The fifth stone is orichalc of which the color is green and within it has as it were golden drops. And its power is to defend a man from the gallows. And its virtue is that it makes one to prophecy things to come if it were in the hand and kept clean and chaste. And its figure is the image of an ass.

The sixth stone is sapphire the color of which is fully blue and fair as heaven. Its power is that it heals all infirmities that increase in a man of inflammation or problems of the eyes. And it cleanses them much. And if in this stone be graven the head of a man with a beard, it delivers a man from prison and from all pressure. And this stone accords to the power of great Lords and of kings. If this stone be kept cleanly, reverently, and chastely and that it be from the orient, with it a man might attain great honor, and the profit of it that he seeks. And its symbol is that of Aries.

The seventh stone is beryl the color of which is of the eye or of sea water, and some of them be round and some are in a pentagonal shape. This stone ought to be clear within and clean, and its power is to keep the hand closed of him that bears it. And if it be set in gold it gives great friendship betwixt two men if you touch the man with it. And its figure is Rana, that is a frog, and it is of great power for to make peace concord & love.

The eighth stone is onyx. this stone is full black, and its power is to give him that bears it many dreadful dreams and nightmares. He that sees himself in it has power upon all devils in constraining them and in conjuring them forth, conjuring as is needed. And its figure is the head of a camel or two heads betwixt two trees of the type called mirti.

The ninth stone is called carnelian the color of which is red and fair, and its power is to make other stones fairer. Its virtue is to give good color to him that bears it, and it is put in gold. And if there be graven in it *Aquila,* that is, an eagle, it gives great honor.

The tenth stone is chrysolite, and it is of golden green color and sparkles like a fire. Its power is to gather together devils and winds. And its virtue is to defend the place where it is from evil spirits and dead men that they do not dwell therein. And devils will obey one with this stone. And its figure is a vulture.

The eleventh stone is called bloodstone. And it is a stone of great power of which the color is green and fair with red drops inside like drops of blood. This stone is called the stone of wise men, of prophets, and of philosophers. And this is honored for two things; for the color like to emerald in its greens, and like ruby in its red. The price of this stone overcomes the price of all others, and of its virtues and proprieties. the power of this stone is that if it be put in any broad vessel full of water in the sun it vaporizes the water. And it makes it to be raised upward till that into the rain it is converted, thus coming back down as such. Its virtue is that who that bears it in the mouth or in the hand closed he may not be seen of any man. With this stone a man may have power upon all devils and make each incantation or enchantment that he desires. And in this stone ought to be graven the evening star.

The twelfth stone is quartz of which the color is white like ice. Its power is that it puts out the power of fire from it. And its virtue is that it increases and nourishes the body and does much good. And you may take in it what virtue you desire. After that the hour shall be in which you have wrought. And after that the magic from it will be whatever you have deemed it to be. Know that it has many virtues. And its figure is a griffon.

The thirteenth stone is cornelian and it is like water and blood, or the washing of blood. And its power is to stanch out bleeding. And on this must be graven a man in a robe with a staff, and it gives honor to him that bears it.

The fourteenth stone is jasper and it is thick, dark, and green with red, and if there be some clear spots in it the stone is better than the rest. And also if there are some thick red drops within it. And its power is that whoever bears it, is not subjected to poisoning by snake or spider, neither with scorpion, and it defends a man from a fever if in it be graven Leo, Aries, or Sagittarius.

The fifteenth stone is Iris (A prism) and it is likened to crystal or to gelatin, and it has to be carved with corners, and if any man put it in an house within the sun s that it shines through the stone, the color changes to that of a rainbow. And for this it is said of Iris stone that is the rainbow stone. And this is its might; for it has seven corners. And the virtue of it is to keep the place in which it is with health and honesty, and there ought to be graven in it a man with a bow and arrow.

The sixteenth stone is coral and it grows in the riches of the sea as in a harbor, looking like the roots of a tree. And it has branches as a tree like that of a palm. And when it is drawn up it is green and tender, and when it is dried in the air, it is made red and hard as another stone and sometimes it is found white. And know that the red coral be better. And where this stone is kept it keeps the home and vineyard free from disasters or sickness and defends against malevolent enchantment. And its image is a man like to him that has a sword in hand.

The seventeenth stone is prossin and it is of a green color, and thick and fair, and it helps everyone and gives the grace of angelic ministry and Taurus ought to be graven in it.

The eighteenth stone is called catel and it is of great power both in deed and virtue. The color of it is like beryl, but for it is darker and has beams or streaks within it. And there be found some of six corners and some of five. And its power is to subjugate demons so they can be spoken to. And its virtue is, that if you bring some river water and bring to a road the stone hanged upon the neck of an ass fumigated with mastic, thur, and croco, and you speak to a dead man there, he will tell you what you wish to know. Know that he will appear to you then. And engrave a lapwing upon the stone with, on the reverse, the tree called mimosa.

The nineteenth stone is tortoise shell and it is green as an herb. Its power is that it increases and decreases like the phases of the moon. And its power is to make peace and harmony between people if on it is carved the figure of a swallow.

The twentieth stone is chalcedony and it is white and opaque. Its power is to overcome sickness. Its virtue is to hold a man from harm in an alien land. And its image is a man that holds his right hand straight forth to heaven.

The twenty first stone is cerannus. This stone is of many colors and comes from many places. Sometimes it is green, sometimes white, sometimes red or brown. And some places it appears like iron, elsewhere like copper or sulfur, and it sometimes appears as little droplets. And its power is to defend a place from lightning. And its virtue is to defend from all enemies. And write on one side of it Raphael, Michael, Gabriel. And on the other side Pantaseron, Micracon. Saidalson. And when you bear it you may overcome all enemies.

The twenty second stone is amethyst and it has the color of wine upon a white cloth or of rose, or violet. And this has might to chase away fiends. And its virtue is to defend from drunkenness. And its figure is Ursa, that is, a bear.

The twenty third stone is magnetite. And it is of great weight and like to brown iron. Its power is that it is able to draw iron close to it. And its virtue is that with it you might be in what house you wish and do what you wish with other men, and with things of the house, fumigating the home and with other enchantments. And engrave a seven armed man upon it, when Luna is in Aries, or Scorpio is joined to Mars. And make sure the Sun is beholding them. And know that you may enchant the same with any image to represent what you wish from it.

The twenty fourth stone is adamas and it is of gray color and the best pieces are slightly green. And its power is that with it other stones be engraved, and therefore it is stronger than they, and more magical. And its power or virtue is to keep the members of a man safe and whole. And this stone is more and better itself at price in enchantments and in invocations of winds, spirits, or devils. And with this you may send whatever fantasy you wish. And its figure is of five corners. And know each man who that bear with him such a stone, he must be pure and clean, when he would do any thing with them. Let him avoid uncleanliness and keep the stone reverently in a clean niche. And Raziel said in the hour in which you work from Semiphoras, bear the three stones above said and you will profit." (p. 28-34.)

SIGNS, OMENS, AND SUPERSTITIONS
Astra Cielo, 1918.

"Precious Stones

Precious stones are supposed in all countries to have a special province in inducing fortunate or unlucky occurrences. The proper stone is chosen according to the month of one's birth, each month being governed by a different gem. The following is the list of birth stones according to the generally accepted belief:

January, Garnet
February, Amethyst
March, Bloodstone
April, Diamond
May, Emerald
June, Agate
July, Ruby
August, Sardonyx
September, Sapphire
October, Opal
November, Topaz
December, Turquoise

A ring presented to a person with his or her birthstone is sure to bring good fortune. One's birthstone in a charm or locket, worn about the neck, will bring luck in business or speculation." (p. 84-85.)

THE POWER OF GEMS AND CHARMS
Geo Bratley, 1906

"The Language of Precious Stones

The following list will give the attributed virtues of those gems used for jewelry, and are those mostly worn for this purpose at the present day.

Agate: This stone is cooling and allays fevers, quenches thirst, and quiets the pulse and heart throbs, insures good health and a long and prosperous life. They are also said by the ancients to render their wearer invisible. Bound on the horns of oxen will give a good harvest.

Amber: Is excellent for the fires of the soul, for the eyes, and for glandular swellings of the throat and lungs. It insures the wearer good luck, and a very long enjoyment of the qualities which make the wearer attractive.

Amethyst: This is a sure averter of drunkenness; it preserves from strong passions, and brings peace of mind; it promotes chastity, and will strengthen the will power. In battle it renders the wearer brave, far-seeing, and honorable.

Ammonite: It is used in the religious ceremonies of the Hindus, and is said, if placed near the deathbed of one dying, to introduce his soul to the deities.

Beryl: Used by the South Sea Islanders as a rainmaker, and said to be equally efficacious in bringing drought on their enemies.

Bezoar or Beza: A charm against plague and poison, Tavenier, the traveler, in his works, mentions this stone, and how to tell the true from the counterfeit, he says, 'There are two infallible tests; one is to place it in the mouth, and if it is genuine it will give a leap and fix itself on the palate; the other consists in placing the stone in a glass of water, and if true bezoar the water will boil.'

Bloodstone: Gives courage, success, and wisdom in perilous undertakings. In the West Indies it is used for the cure of wounds, being wetted in cold water, and in magical works it is used in incantations. A favorite stone with the Gnostics, who employed it largely in their gems and talismans. Also called the heliotrope.

Bufonite: Cures the bite of snakes and other poisonous reptiles.

Carbuncle: Corrects evils resulting from mistaken friendships; it holds to the owner the passionate love of all those whose love may be desired.

Cornelian or Cornelian: Gives content and friendship. Promotes astral vision.

Cat's Eye: A charm against witchcraft. It is lucky and possesses the virtue of enriching the wearer. Same as the chrysoberyl.

Chrysolite: Cures madness and despair, banishes misfortune, and gives hope.

Coral: Guards against evil. It is used in difficulties of the heart, lungs, and in indigestion; it excites nerve power, brilliancy and gladness, sund is a true health-giver.

Crystal: Brings calm, sweet sleep, and good dreams; it enables the inner soul to hear the silent voice of the oracle and to foretell future events.

Diamond: Gives faith, purity, life, joy, innocence, and repentance. Good for developing concentration and to promote spiritual ecstasy. Loses its brilliancy with the health of the wearer, and only regains it when the owner recovers. Capable of detecting poisons by exhibiting a moisture or perspiration on its surface.

Emerald: Gives faith; success in love, discovers false friends, promotes constancy of mind and warm, true friendship, felicity in domestic life. It changes color when false friends or false witnesses are near, and as a love token it registers the degree of love. If it is pale, then love is waning; if it loses color entirely, the lover is false and the love gone for ever. Its soft green color has a beneficial effect upon the wearer's own eyes, and is a good talisman for any eye trouble; but serpents are said to become blind if they even look at an emerald. If worn about the neck or finger is efficacious against fits and prevents convulsions in children.

Garnet: Constancy and fidelity in every engagement; gives cheerfulness and the ability to hold one's own in the world. If worn out of season promotes discord between lovers.

Hyacinth: Worn on the neck or finger will preserve the wearer from infection even if he go into an infected place; gives honor, the support and esteem of superiors.

Jade: A powerful bringer of luck. All Chinese have a great belief in its fortune-bestowing powers.

Jasper: Courage, wisdom, and firmness; success in dangerous enterprises.

Lodestone: Will increase the mental powers, and enables the wearer to foretell future events.

Malachite: Brilliant success and happiness in every

circumstance of life.

Moonstone: Protects from harm and danger; very cooling in fever if applied to both temples. Good fortune in love matters.

Olivine: Frees the mind from sadness and evil passions.

Onyx: Disturbs the slumbers and the mind; gives frightful dreams.

Opal: Denotes hope and good fortune; it sharpens the sight and strengthens the faith of the possessor. The fiery opal possesses the united virtues of all the gems into whose distinctive hues it is emblazoned: the ruby's strength and courage; blue, the prosperity of the turquoise; green, the emerald's faithfulness, and so with the other colors. It has long been a superstition that the opal is an unlucky stone to wear, but its original significance was good luck. It may safely be worn if it is the stone of the birth-month, or if one's birthstone is worn at the same time. If these rules are not observed, it is fatal to love and will break friendships, also the female wearing it will bear no children.

Ophite: Gives the power to see visions and hear the voices of the invisible.

Pearl: Gives purity and innocence, also clearness to physical and mental sight. The pearl's beauty depends much on the health of the wearer.

Peridot: Cheers the mind, prevents irritability, and removes depression.

Ruby: Divine power, love, dignity, and royalty. Holds to the owner the love of those loved; corrects evils resulting from mistaken friendships; discovers poison; will quicken the blood and increase the will of the animal body, and will give vivacity; will cause obstacles to melt away, and inspire with bravery and zeal. It will bring one's due in money that has been misappropriated.

Sapphire: Truth and constancy, denotes repentance; frees from enchantment; signifies piety and goodness; insures protection against many diseases, and will warn of hidden dangers. If the possessor wears it in any haunt of dissipation his actions will at once be known to the one he holds dearest.

Sardonyx: Gives conjugal felicity, favors fortune. The woman whose stone it is and who neglects to wear it is doomed to a lonely existence.

Snakestone: Renders its possessor invulnerable against the bite of snakes.

Stone-of-Memphis: Applied to any part of the body on which it is necessary for the surgeon to operate upon it preserves that part from any pain in the operation.

Tiger's Eye: A lucky stone; it enriches the wearer.

Topaz: Fidelity in friendship; prevents bad dreams; cheers the wearer; strengthens the intellect; brightens the wit; protects against the perils of the sea; will lose its color in the presence of poisons; gives nerve strength, and helps the heart and digestion.

Turquoise: Success, happiness, and many friends; prosperity in love, and obtains friends as is verified by the old saying: 'He who possesses a turquoise will always be sure of friends.' If given by a lover, it will lose its color should the love wane, or will change color if danger threatens the wearer.

The twelve foundations of the New Jerusalem are

supposed to represent as many apostolic virtues, such as:

1. Amethyst: Sobriety and temperance.
2. Beryl: Goodness of mind at all times.
3. Chalcedony: Ardent zeal.
4. Chrysolite: Restrained by no obstacles.
5. Chrysoprase: Severity towards sin.
6. Emerald: Suavity of manner.
7. Jasper: Firmness and constancy
8. Hyacinth: Calmness in all things.
9. Sapphire: Heavenly and beautiful thoughts.
10. Sardius: Readiness for martyrdom.
11. Sardonyx: Variety in teaching.
12. Topaz: Healing power." (p. 67-72.)

SUMMONING AND DEFEATING SPIRITS

ARS GOETIA
Samuel Mathers (trans.), 1904

"The Magical Circle:

This is the form of the magical circle of King Solomon, the which he made that he might preserve himself therein from the malice of these Evil Spirits. This magical circle is to be made 9 feet across, and the divine names are to be written around it, beginning at EHYEH, and ending at LEVANAH, Luna. It must be colored as such: The space between the outer and inner circles, where the serpent is coiled, with the Hebrew names written along his body, is bright deep yellow. The square in the center of the circle, where the word "Master" is written, is filled in with red. All names and letters are in black. In the Hexagrams the outer triangles where the letters A, D, O, N, A, I, appear are filled in with bright yellow, the centers, where the T-shaped crosses are, blue or green. In the Pentagrams outside the circle, the outer triangles where "Te, tra, gram, ma, ton," is written, are filled in bright yellow, and the centers with the T crosses written therein are red.)

The Magical Triangle of Solomon

This is the form of the magical triangle, into the which Solomon did command the evil spirits. It is to be made at 2 feet distance from the magical circle and it is 3 feet across. Note that this triangle is to be placed toward that quarter to which the spirit belongs. And the base of the triangle is to be nearest unto the circle, the apex pointing in the direction of the quarter of the spirit. Observe also the Moon in this working, as aforesaid, etc. It must be colored as such: Triangle outlined in black; name of Michael black on white ground; the three names without the triangle written in red; circle in center entirely filled in in dark green." (p. 88-90.)

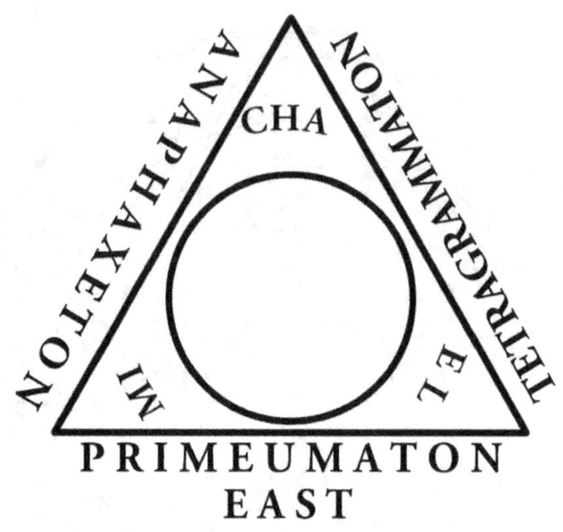

Note: These preceding entries are the two basic components needed to work all of the basic summoning rituals within the Ars Goetia, one of the books of the Lemegeton. The seventy-two demons are individually listed. The first basic conjuration follows.

"The Conjuration to Call Forth Any of the Aforesaid Spirits

Please note: with this and subsequent invocations, where "N." appears the name of the spirit is to be stated.

I do invoke and conjure thee, O Spirit, N.; and being with power armed from the SUPREME MAJESTY, I do strongly command thee, by BERALANENSIS, BALDACHIENSIS, PAUMACHIA, and APOLOGIAE SEDES; by the most powerful Princes, Genii, Liachidee, and Ministers of the Tartarean abode; and by the chief Prince of the Seat of Apologia in the Ninth Legion, I do invoke thee, and by invoking, conjure thee.

And being armed with power from the SUPREME MAJESTY, I do strongly command thee, by Him who spake and it was done, and unto whom all creatures be obedient.

Also I, being made after the image of GOD, endued with power from GOD and created according unto His will, do exorcise thee by that most mighty and powerful name of GOD, EL, strong and wonderful; O thou Spirit N. And I command thee and Him who spake the word and His FIAT was accomplished, and by all the names of God. Also by the names ADONAI, EL, ELOHIM, ELOHI, EHYEH, ASHER EHYEH, ZABAOTH, ELION, IAH, TETRAGRAMMATON, SHADDAI, LORD GOD MOST HIGH, I do exorcise thee and do powerfully command thee, O thou Spirit N., that thou dost forthwith appear unto me here before this circle in a fair human shape, without any deformity or tortuosity. And by this ineffable name, TETRAGRAMMATON IEHOVAH, do I command thee, at the which being heard the elements are overthrown, the air is shaken, the sea runneth back, the fire is quenched, the earth trembleth, and all the hosts of the celestials, terrestrials, and infernals, do tremble together, and are troubled and confounded.

Wherefore come thou, O Spirit N., forthwith, and without delay, from any or all parts of the world wherever thou mayest be, and make rational answers unto all things that I shall demand of thee. Come thou peaceably, visibly, and affably, now, and without delay, manifesting that which I shall desire. For thou art conjured by the name of the LIVING and TRUE GOD, HELIOREN, wherefore fulfill thou my commands, and persist thou therein unto the end, and according unto mine interest, visibly and affably speaking unto me with a voice clear and intelligible without any ambiguity." (p. 97-98.)

ASSAMESE DEMONOLOGY
Benudhar Rajkhowa, 1906

"(a) Karsala Ban: Karsala is a kind of grass. The possessed man is struck with this grass, duly enchanted. The spirit then makes his retreat.

(b) Guburua Ban: Literally a 'beetle arrow.' Three beetles are killed and squeezed to powder, and are then mixed ceremonially with mustard oil and alkaline water. This mixture, sprinkled on the body; of the possessed man, expels the spirit.

(c) Agni Ban: Literally 'fire arrow.' A torch is prepared of titabahak twigs, the flame being held up. A quantity of mustard seed is thrown over the fire in such manner that sparks are let off and fall on the body of the possessed man, the usual incantations being repeated in the meantime.

(d) Jal Ban: Literally 'water arrow'. The rib of a dried plantain leaf is burnt to ashes which are mixed with a quantity of bubble-bubble water. The mixture being sprinkled on the eyes (if the possessed man with proper incantations makes the spirit retire.

(e) Kharika Ban: Literally 'arrow of thatching grass.' A quantity of thatching grass is enchanted and cast on the body of the possessed man, when the spirit runs away.

(f) Bishnu Ban: Garlic, onion and certain other medicinal roots are pulverized, and mixed with mustard oil and and water. The mixture is sprinkled on the body of the possessed man with proper incantations. The spirit then leaves the victim and repairs to his haunt.

(g) Sariah Ban: Literally 'mustard arrow.' The exorcist takes a quantity of mustard seeds in his mouth and blows them towards the possessed man through a sieve placed in front of him, uttering certain incantations mean while. The mustard falling on the possessed man causes a burning sensation. The spirit unable to bear the pain leaves his victim.

(h) Kher Ban: Literally 'straw arrow.' A quantity of straw duly enchanted is thrown at the possessed man. This, when it hits him, makes the spirit fly for life.

(i) Rudra Ban: Mustard seeds, orris and certain other medicinal roots are pulverized and mixed diluted with mustard oil. The mixture when sprinkled on the man's eyes makes the spirit depart to the place from Which it came.

(j) Chakra Ban: The mode of exorcism is much the same as the above. In time of emergency the exorcist uses only short incantations called dikhas. The following dikhas are in use: Sani Dikha, Kal Dikha, Rudra Dikha, Nara Dikha, Singha Dikha, Brahma Dikha." (p. 18-19.)

THE GRAND GRIMOIRE
1750

"Great Invocation to Summon the Spirit with whom one wishes to the pact excerpted from The Great Clavicle:

'Emperor LUCIFER, master of all the rebel spirits, I ask you to be favorable in my summons of your Great Minister LUCIFUGE ROFOCALE, since I wish to make a pact with him. I also request that you, Prince BELZEBUTH, protect me in my undertaking; O Come ASTAROTH be propitious and ensure that the great LUCIFUGE appears to me tonight in human guise and without emitting foul odors and he grant me as per the pact that I will present to him, all of the riches which I require. O great LUCIFUGE, I request that you abandon your dwelling, in whatever part of the world it should be, to come and speak with me. Otherwise, I will force you by the power of the great living

God and his dear Son and the Holy Spirit: obey now, or I will eternally torment you by the authority of the powerful words of Solomon's great Clavicle of which he made use to oblige the rebel Spirits to receive his pact; therefore, appear as quickly as possible or I will continually torment you by the authority of the powerful words of the Clavicle:

Aglon, Tetragram, vaycheon stimulamaton ezphares Tetragrammaton, olyaramirion esytion existion eryona onera orasim mozm messias soter Emanuel Sabaoth ADONAY, te adoro et te invoco. Amen.'

You can be certain that before having finished reading the above mentioned powerful words the spirit will appear and will tell you the following.

Apparition of the Spirit:

'Here I am. What would you ask of me? Why do you torment my rest? Answer me!'

-Lucifuge Rofocale

Request to the Spirit:

'I may ask you to make a pact with me so that you make me rich as soon as possible, otherwise I will torment you by the powerful words of the Clavicle.'

-Karcist

Response of the Spirit:

'I can not grant your request except on the condition that you give yourself to me for the next 20 years so that I can use your body and soul as I see fit.'

-Lucifuge Rofocale

Then you will throw him your pact, which must be in your hand writing on a sheet of virgin parchment, which will consist of these few words, with your signature written in your blood. Here is the pact:

'I promise to repay the great Lucifuge in 20 years for all of the treasures that he will give me. On my honor I sign this in good faith.'

Your signature here must be signed in blood.

Response of the Spirit:

'I can not grant your request.'

-Lucifuge Rofocale

Second Appearance of the Spirit:

Then, in order to force the spirit to obey you, re-read the great Invocation of the terrible words of the Clavicle, until the spirit appears and tells you the following:

'Why do you torment me more and more? If you leave me in peace, I will give you the nearest treasure on the condition that you consecrate a coin to me all of the Mondays of every month and that you will call me one day every week, from ten o'clock in the evening until 2 two in the morning. Take your pact which I have signed; and if you do not maintain your word you will be mine in 20 years.'

-Lucifuge Rofocale

Response to the Spirit:

'I adhere to your demands, on the condition that you enable me to have the nearest treasure and that I can take it with me right away.'

-Karcist

Response of the Spirit:

'Follow me and take the treasure that I am going to show you.'

-Lucifuge Rofocale

Then follow the spirit on the path to the treasure that will be indicated (at the triangle) without taking fright and throw the signed pact over the treasure and touching it with the rod take as much of it as you can. Then return inside the triangle, making certain to walk backwards, where you will deposit your treasure in front of yourself, dismissing the spirit as follows:

The Conjuring and Dismissal of the Spirit with whom the pact is made:

'O great LUCIFUGE, I am satisfied with you at present; I will leave you to peace and permit you to retire to wherever you wish without making any noise or leaving any bad odors. Think then, about your duty regarding my pact; since, if the one instant you shirk your obligation, you can be sure that I will torment you eternally with the great and powerful words of the great Clavicle of the great King Solomon with which he forced all of the rebel spirits to obey him.'

Prayer to the Omnipotent in Thanksgiving:

'Omnipotent God, heavenly father, who created all things for the service and use of man, I humbly thank you, that in your great goodness and that you have permitted that I could make a pact with a spirit that is a rebel of your authority and subdue it to obey me in fulfilling all of my needs. I thank you, O omnipotent God, for the good that you have done me tonight to have shown myself to be worthy to have granted to me, miserable creature, your precious favors and to present, great God, now that I have come to know the force and power of your great promises, when you said: 'seek and you shall find', 'knock and the door shall be opened' as you have recommended to raise the poor, condescend O great God to inspire me to true sentiment of charity so that I can spread with this Great Work a great portion of the possessions your great divinity permitted that I could receive. Let it be, O great God, that I can enjoy these great riches that I possess, with tranquility and do not permit any rebel spirit to harm my enjoyment of these precious treasures over which you permit me to own. Inspire in me, O great God, the necessary sentiment to unbind me from the grips of the devil and all maleficent spirits. I trust, O great God, in the Father, the Son, and the Holy Spirit and in your saintly protection. Amen.' (p. 31-34.)

GRIMOIRE OF POPE HONORIUS
1760

"Universal Conjuration:

'I, N., do conjure thee, O Spirit N., by the living God, by the true God, by the holy and all-ruling God, who created from nothingness the heaven, the earth, the sea, and all things that are therein, in virtue of the Most Holy Sacrament of the Eucharist, in the name of Jesus Christ, and by the power of this same Almighty Son of God, who for us and for our redemption was crucified, suffered death, and was buried; who rose again on the third day, and is now seated on the right hand of the Creator of the whole world, from whence he will come to judge the living and the dead; as also by the precious love of the Holy Spirit, perfect Trinity. I conjure thee within the circle, accursed one, by thy judgment, who didst dare to tempt God: I exorcise thee, Serpent, and I command thee to appear forthwith under a beautiful and well-favored human form of soul and body, and to fulfill my behests without any deceit whatsoever, as also without mental reservation of any kind, by the great times of the God of gods and Lord of lords, ADONAY, TETRAGRAMMATON, JEHOVA, TETRAGRAMMATON, ADONAY, JEHOVA, OTHEOS, ATHANATOS, ISCHYROS, AGLA, PENTAGRAMMATON, SADAY, SADAY, SADAY, JEHOVA, OTHEOS, ATHANATOS, ALICIAT, TETRAGRAMMATON, ADONAY, ISCHYROS, ATHANATOS, SADY, SADY, SADY, CADOS, CADOS, CADOS, ELOY, AGLA, AGLA, AGLA, ADONAY, ADONAY. I conjure thee, Evil and Accursed Serpent, N.. to appear at my will and pleasure, in this place, before this circle, without tarrying, without companions, without grievance, without noise, deformity, or murmuring. I exorcise thee by the ineffable names of God, to wit, Gog and Magog, which I am unworthy to pronounce; Come hither, Conic hither, Come hither. Accomplish my will and desire, without wile or falsehood. Otherwise St. Michael, the invisible Archangel, shall presently blast thee in the utmost depths of hell. Come, then, N., to do my will.'" (p. 12.)

GRIMORIUM VERUM
18th Century

"To Make Three Men or Women Appear

It is necessary to be chaste for three days before these workings.

On the fourth day, as soon as it is morning, clean and prepare your room, as soon as you have dressed yourself. You must be fasting during this process. Make sure that your room will not be disturbed for the whole of this fourth day. There should be nothing hanging, nor crossing the room, no tapestries or curtains or clothes hanging about the area, nor hats, bird cages, bed curtains, and such. Above all, make sure that everything is clean as much as possible.

Ceremony:

After you have eaten, go secretly to your room, which you have cleaned. Upon the table, set a white cloth and three chairs. In front of each chair, set a loaf of wheat bread and a glass of water. Now place a chair at your bedside and lay upon the bed, and say the following:

Conjuration:

'Besticitum confolatio veni ad me vertat Creon, Creon, Creon, cantor laudem omnipotentis et non commentur. Stat superior carta bient laudem omviestra principiem da montem et inimicos meos o prostantis vobis et mihi dantes que passium fieri sincisibus.'

The three people, having arrived, will sit by the fire eating and drinking, and will thank you for having entertained them. If you are a man, three girls will come, but if you are a female, three young men will come. Then the three will draw lots as to which will stay with you. If the operator is male, the girl who wins will sit in the chair which you have placed by your bedside and will stay with you until midnight. At this time she will leave with her companions, all without having been dismissed, the two others remaining by the fire while the third entertains you. While she is with you, you may ask her any question about any art or science, or any other subject, and she will immediately give you her reply. You can ask where treasure is hidden, and she will tell you where it is and how it may be obtained. If the treasure is guarded by demonic forces, she and her companions will accompany you and guard you against them.

When she leaves she will give you a ring. If you wear this on your finger you will be fortunate while gambling. If you place the ring on the finger or any woman you will be immediately able to obtain what you wish from her. Your window, it should be noted, is to be left open during this process. You may perform this experiment as often as you wish." (p. 16-17.)

THE ART OF DRAWING SPIRITS INTO CRYSTALS
Trithemius, 16th Century

"Of the Making of the Crystal and the Form of Preparation in a Vision

Procure of a lapidary good clear pellucid crystal, of the size of a small orange, or about one inch and a half in diameter; let it be globular or round and as evenly so as possible; then, when you have obtained this crystal, fair and clear, without any clouds or specks, get a small plate of pure gold to encompass the crystal round one half; let this be fitted on an ivory or ebony pedestal, as you may see more fully described in the drawing.

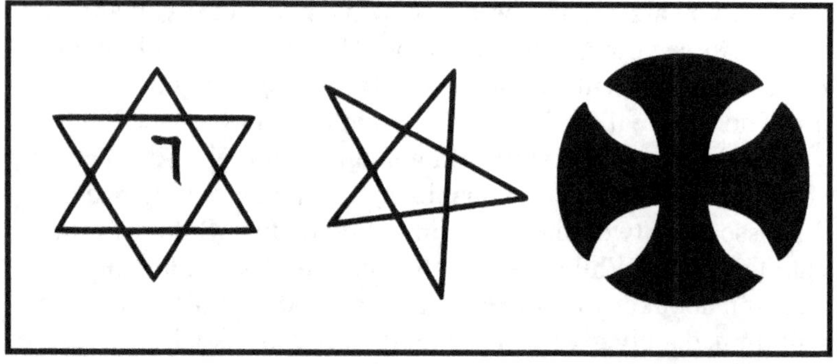

Let there be engraved a circle round the crystal with these characters around inside the circle next the crystal and afterwards the name 'Tetragrammaton.' On the other side of the plate let there be engraved 'Michael, Gabriel, Uriel, Raphael;'

which are the four principal angels ruling over the Sun, Moon, Venus and Mercury; but on the table on which the crystal stands the following names, characters, and such. must be drawn in order.

First, the names of the seven planets and angels ruling them, with their seals or characters. The names of the four kings of the four corners of the earth. Let them be all written within a double circle, with a triangle on a table; on which place the crystal on its pedestal: this being done, the table is complete (as in the Fig. D,) and fit for the calling of the spirits; after which you may proceed to experiment, thus:

In what time you wish to deal with the spirits by the table and crystal, you must observe the planetary hour; and whatever planet rules in that hour, the angel governing the planet you may call in the manner following; but first, say this short prayer:

'Oh, God! who art the author of all good things, strengthen, I beseech thee, thy poor servant, that he may stand fast, without fear, through this dealing and work. Enlighten, I beseech thee, oh Lord! the dark understanding of thy creature, so that his spiritual eye may be opened to see and know thy angelic spirits descending here in this crystal: (then lay thy hand on the crystal saying,) and thou, oh inanimate creature of God, be sanctified and consecrated, and blessed to this purpose, that no evil fantasy may appear in thee; or, if they do gain ingress into this creature, they may be constrained to speak intelligibly, and truly, and without the least ambiguity, for Christ's sake. Amen. And inasmuch as thy servant here standing before thee, oh, Lord! desires neither evil treasures, nor injury to his neighbor, nor hurt to any living creature, grant him the power of descrying those celestial spirits or intelligences, that may appear in this crystal, and whatever good gifts, whether the power of healing infirmities, or of imbibing wisdom, or discovering any evil likely to afflict any person or family, or any other good gift thou mayest be pleased to bestow on me, enable me, by thy wisdom and mercy, to use whatever I may receive to the honor of thy holy name. Grant this for thy son Christ's sake. Amen.'

Then taking your ring and pentacle, put the ring on the little finger of your right hand; hang the pentacle round your neck; (note, the pentacle may be either wrote on clean virgin parchment, or engraved on a square plate of silver and suspended from your neck to the breast,) then take your black ebony wand, with the gilt characters on it and trace the circle, (Fig. 7. C D E F,) saying as such;

'In the name of the blessed Trinity, I consecrate this piece of ground for our defense; so that no evil spirit may have power to break these bounds prescribed here, through Jesus Christ our Lord. Amen.'

Then place the vessel for the perfumes between your circle and the holy table on which the crystal stands, and, having fire therein, cast in your perfumes, saying;

'I conjure thee, oh thou creature of fire! by him who created all things both in heaven and earth, and in the sea, and in every other place whatever, that forthwith thou cast away every phantasm from thee, that no hurt whatsoever shall be done in any thing. Bless, oh Lord, this creature of fire, and sanctify it that it may be blessed, and that they may fill up the power and virtue of their odors; so neither the enemy, nor any false imagination, may enter into them; through our Lord Jesus Christ. Amen.'

Now, this being done in the order prescribed, take out your little book, which must be made about seven inches long, of pure white virgin vellum or paper, likewise pen and ink must be ready to write down the name, character, and office, likewise the seal or image of whatever spirit may appear- for this I must tell you that it does not happen that the same spirit you call will always appear, for you must try the spirit to know whether he be a pure or impure being, and this you will easily know by a firm and undoubted faith in God.

Now the most pure and simple way of calling the spirits or spirit is by a short oration to the spirit himself, which is more effectual and easy to perform than composing a table of letters; for all celestial operations, the more pure and unmixed they are, the more they are agreeable to the celestial spirits: Therefore, after the circle is drawn, the book, perfumes, rod, and such, in readiness, proceed as follows:

After noticing the exact hour of the day, and what angel rules that hour, you shall say;

'In the name of the blessed and holy Trinity, I do desire thee, thou strong mighty angel, Michael, (Or any other angel or spirit) that if it be the divine will of him who is called Tetragrammaton, the Holy God, the Father, that thou take upon thee some shape as best becomes thy celestial nature, and appear to us visibly here in this crystal, and answer our demands in as far as we shall not transgress the bounds of the divine mercy and goodness, by requesting unlawful knowledge; but that thou wilt graciously shew us what things are most profitable for us to know and do, to the glory and honor of his divine Majesty, who liveth and reigneth, world without end. Amen.'

'Lord, thy will be done on earth, as it is in heaven; make clean our hearts within us, and take not thy Holy Spirit from us.'

'O Lord, by thy name, we have called him, suffer him to administer unto us. And that all things may work together for thy honor and glory, to whom with thee, the Son, and blessed Spirit, be ascribed all might, majesty and dominion. Amen'

Note, In these dealings, two should always be present; for often a spirit is manifest to one in the crystal when the other cannot perceive him; therefore if any spirit appear, as there most likely will, to one or both, say,

'Oh, Lord! we return thee our hearty and sincere thanks for the hearing of our prayer, and we thank thee for having permitted thy spirit to appear unto us which we, by thy mercy, will interrogate to our further instruction, through Christ. Amen.'

Interrogation in the name of the holy and undefiled Spirit, the Father, the begotten Son, and Holy Ghost, proceeding from both; 'What is thy true name?'

If the spirit answers, Michael, then proceed.

Question 2: 'What is thy office?' 3: 'What is thy true sign or character?' 4: 'When are the times most agreeable to thy nature to hold conference with us?'

'Wilt thou swear by the blood and righteousness of our Lord Jesus Christ, that thou art truly Michael?'

Here let him swear, then write down his seal or character in your book, and against it, his office and times to be called, through God's name; also write down any thing he may teach you or any responses he may make to your questions or interrogations, concerning life or death, arts or sciences, or any other thing, and then say;

'Thou great and mighty spirit, inasmuch as thou camest in peace and in the name of the ever blessed and righteous Trinity, so in this name thou mayest depart, and return to us when we call thee in his name to whom every knee doth bow down. Fare thee well, Michael; peace be between us, through our blessed Lord Jesus Christ. Amen.' Then will the spirit depart; then say; 'To God the Father, eternal Spirit, fountain of Light, the Son, and Holy Ghost, be all honor and glory, world without end. Amen.' I shall here set down the table of the names of Spirits and Planets governing the Hours; so you will easily know by inspection, what Spirit and Planet governs every Hour of the Day and Night in the Week.

SUNDAY

Hour of the day	Hour of the night
1 Michael	1 Sachiel
2 Anael	2 Samael
3 Raphael	3 Michael
4 Gabriel	4 Anael
5 Cassiel	5 Raphael
6 Sachiel	6 Gabriel
7 Samael	7 Cassiel
8 Michael	8 Sachiel
9 Anael	9 Samael
10 Raphael	10 Michael
11 Gabriel	11 Anael
12 Cassiel	12 Raphael

MONDAY

Hour of the day	Hour of the night
1 Gabriel	1 Anael
2 Cassiel	2 Raphael
3 Sachiel	3 Gabriel
4 Samael	4 Cassiel
5 Michael	5 Sachiel
6 Anael	6 Samael
7 Raphael	7 Michael
8 Gabriel	8 Anael
9 Cassiel	9 Raphael
10 Sachiel	10 Gabriel
11 Samael	11 Cassiel
12 Michael	12 Sachiel

TUESDAY

Hour of the day	Hour of the night
1 Samael	1 Cassiel
2 Michael	2 Sachiel
3 Anael	3 Samael
4 Raphael	4 Michael
5 Gabriel	5 Anael
6 Cassiel	6 Raphael
7 Sachiel	7 Gabriel
8 Samael	8 Cassiel
9 Michael	9 Sachiel
10 Anael	10 Samael
11 Raphael	11 Michael
12 Gabriel	12 Anael

WEDNESDAY

Hour of the day	Hour of the night
1 Raphael	1 Michael
2 Gabriel	2 Anael
3 Cassiel	3 Raphael
4 Sachael	4 Gabriel
5 Samael	5 Cassiel
6 Michael	6 Sachiel
7 Anael	7 Samael
8 Raphael	8 Michael
9 Gabriel	9 Anael
10 Cassiel	10 Raphael
11 Sachiel	11 Gabriel
12 Samael	12 Cassiel

THURSDAY

Hour of the day	Hour of the night
1 Sachiel	1 Gabriel
2 Samael	2 Cassiel
3 Michael	3 Sachiel
4 Anael	4 Samael
5 Raphael	5 Michael
6 Gabriel	6 Anael
7 Cassiel	7 Raphael
8 Sachiel	8 Gabriel
9 Samael	9 Cassiel
10 Michael	10 Sachiel
11 Anael	11 Samael
12 Raphael	12 Michael

FRIDAY

Hour of the day	Hour of the night
1 Anael	1 Samael
2 Raphael	2 Michael
3 Gabriel	3 Anael
4 Cassiel	4 Raphael
5 Sachiel	5 Gabriel
6 Samael	6 Cassiel
7 Michael	7 Sachiel
8 Anael	8 Samael
9 Raphael	9 Michael
10 Gabriel	10 Anael
11 Cassiel	11 Raphael
12 Sachiel	12 Gabriel

SATURDAY

Hour of the day	Hour of the night
1 Cassiel	1 Raphael
2 Sachiel	2 Gabrael
3 Samael	3 Cassiel
4 Michael	4 Sachiel
5 Anael	5 Samael
6 Raphael	6 Michael
7 Gabriel	7 Anael
8 Cassiel	8 Raphael
9 Sachiel	9 Gabriel
10 Samael	10 Cassiel
11 Michael	11 Sachiel
12 Anael	12 Samael

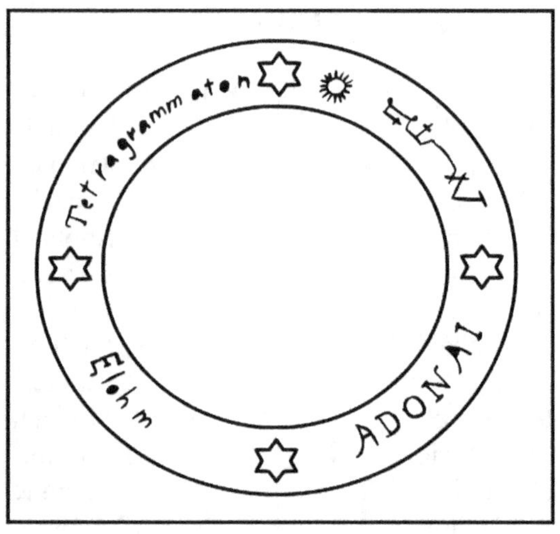

FIGURE 1:

The magickal circle of Michael.

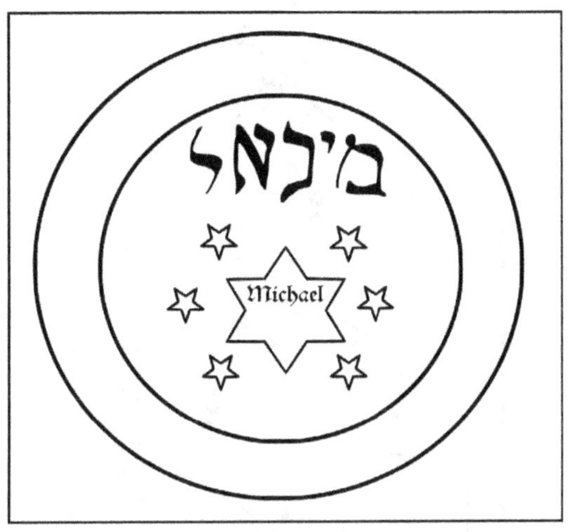

FIGURE 2:

The magickal lamen, to be work by the conjurer: on the outside
rim of the lamen, is inscribed 'El. Elohim. Elohe. Leboath.
Eloim. Echerchie. Adonai. Yah. Jehovah. Tetragrammaton.
Saday. God. Ehevi.'

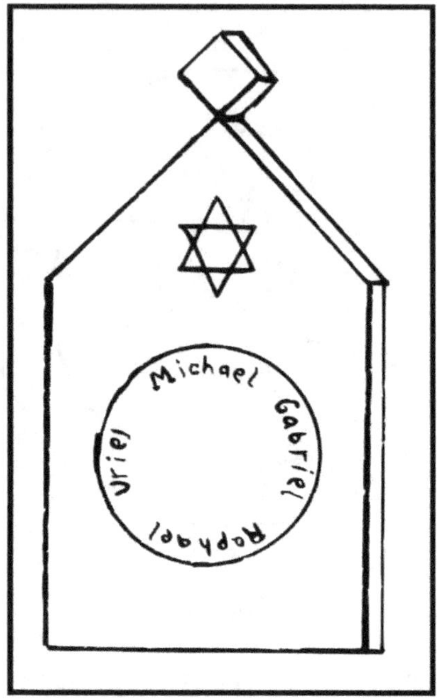

FIGURE 3

The magickal stand in which the crystal is placed, and the stand, of ebony, placed upon the magickal circle of Michael.

FIGURE 4

The wand, used for the conjuring.

(p. 5-24.)

BIBLIOGRAPHY

The following little list of works will help the reader to study these and other various occult topics a bit further, taken from works which I have not personally edited, as the ones included in the present volume are. They are on varied topics, with the titles generally indicative thereof.

Adams, W.H., Davenport, *Witch, Warlock, and Magician*, 1889.

Alexander, W.M., *Demonic Possession in the New Testament*, 1902.

Barrett, Francis, *The Magus, or Celestial Intelligencer*, 1801.

Christian Literature Society for India, *Devil-dancers, Witch-finders, Rain-makers and Medicine-men*, 1896.

Clodd, Edward, *Magic in Names and in Other Things*, 1921.

Crowley, Aleister, *The Book of Lies*, 1913.

Ennemoser, Joseph, *The History of Magic* (two volumes), 1854.

Evans, Joan, *Magical Jewels of the Middle Ages and the Renaissance, Particularly in England*, 1922.

Garnier, Colonel, The Worship of the Dead, 1909.

Gollansc, Hermann, *The Book of Protection*, 1912.

Grainge, William, *Daemonologia*, 1882.

FOLK MAGIC, SUPERSTITION, AND CHARMS

Greer, John Michael & Warnock, Christopher, *The Complete Picatrix*, 2011.

Haddon, Alfred C., *Magic and Fetishism,* 1906.

Hambly, Wilfrid, *Serpent Worship in Africa*, 1931.

Hatch, David Patterson, *Some More Philosophy of the Hermetics*, 1898.

Hearn, Lafcadio, *In Ghostly Japan*, 1900.

Leland, Charles, *Etruscan Roman Remains*, 1892.

Lewis, Abram, *Paganism Surviving in Christianity*, 1892.

MacKenzie, Williams, *Gaelic Incantations, Charms and Blessings of the Hebrides*, 1896.

Mather, Increase, *The Wonders of the Invisible World*, 1862.

North, H., *A History of the Heathen Mythology*, 1806.

O'Donnell, Elliot, *Werwolves*, 1914.

Philpot, J.H., *The Sacred Tree*, 1897.

Quitman, Henry Frederick, *A Treatise on Magic*, 1810.

Sellon, Edwards, *Annotations on the Sacred Writings of the Hindus*, 1902.

Spence, Lewis, *An Encyclopaedia of Occultism*, 1920.

Summers, Montague, *The Vampire, His Kith and Kin*, 1928.

Waite, Arthur Edward, *The Book of Black Magic and of Pacts*, 1910.

Williams, Howard, *The Superstitions of Witchcraft*, 1865.

Wright, Dudley, *Druidism, the Ancient Faith of Britain*, 1924.

Wright, Thomas, *Narratives of Sorcery and Magic from the Most Authentic Sources*, 1852.

THE END